Living in Seclusion

棲隱

Living in Seclusion

棲隱

Xiao Xiao

translated by

Ouyang Yu

PUNCHER & WATTMANN

First published in 2022
Published by Puncher and Wattmann
PO Box 279
Waratah NSW 2298

https://www.puncherandwattmann.com
web@puncherandwattmann.com

ISBN   9781922571175

Cover design by
Typesetting by Morgan Arnett
Printed by Lightning Source International

NATIONAL
LIBRARY
OF AUSTRALIA

A catalogue record for this
work is available from the
National Library of Australia

目录　　Contents

潇潇简历

潇潇，诗人、画家，中国诗歌在线总编。1993年主编了中国现代诗编年史丛书《前朦胧诗全集》《朦胧诗全集》《后朦胧诗全集》（1993年四川教育出版社）。出版诗集有：《树下的女人与诗歌》（2005年台海出版社）《踮起脚尖的时间》（2012年作家出版社）《比忧伤更忧伤》（2014年香港类型出版社）《潇潇的诗》（2017年江苏文艺出版社）《Xiao Xiao Poemas》（西班牙语诗集2018年在古巴南方出版社出版，亚瑟夫·阿南达译）《Sad Songs from Another World》（罗马尼亚语诗集2016年在罗马尼亚出版，霍利亚·戈贝译）《水上紫禁宫》（俄语诗集2021年在莫斯科先锋出版社出版，张冰、吴萍、Alekce Filimonov 合译）《忧伤的速度》（韩语诗集2019年11月在韩国抒情诗出版社出版，朴宰雨译）《薏米的种子》（德语诗集，2021年在奥地利出版，顾彬译）等。作品被翻译成德、英、日、法、韩、越南、波斯、阿拉伯、孟加拉、西班牙语等。其绘画作品参加了"中国当代诗人艺术展"；"中国当代文人书画展"等。长诗《另一个世界的悲歌》被评为九十年代女性文学代表作之一（1999年），2018年5月被翻译成英文（欧阳昱译）在英国剑桥《长诗杂志》（Long Pome Magazine））头条全文发表，并受邀到伦敦巴比肯艺术中心图书馆参加《长诗杂志》的发布会和诗歌朗诵。潇潇曾获多项国内外诗歌大奖。如："闻一多诗歌奖"（2014年）、"百年新诗"特别贡献奖（2017年）、《诗潮》年度诗歌奖（2016年）、《北京文学》诗歌奖（2017年）、中国诗歌网2017十大好诗第一名、2018年十佳诗人、罗马尼亚阿尔盖齐国际文学奖（2016年）等。潇潇是第一个获得此奖的亚洲人，并被授予罗马尼亚荣誉市民。2020年，潇潇的词条被收入德国、欧洲最大的文学词典：《外国当代文学批评词典》（Kritisches Lexikon für fremdsprachige Gegenwartsliteratur (KLfG digital) 顾彬撰写。）

About the author

Xiao Xiao is a poet, artist and editor-in-chief of 'China Poetry Online'. In 1993, she edited *A Complete Collection of Pre-menglong Poetry*, *A Complete Collection of Menglong Poetry* and *A Complete Collection of Post-menglong Poetry* (1993). Her published collections of poetry include *The Woman and Her Poetry Under a Tree* (2005), *Time on Tiptoes* (2012), *Sadder than Sadness* (2014), *Xiao Xiao Poemas* (translated by Versiones de Yasef Ananda and published 2018 in Spanish in Cuba), *Sad Songs from Another World* (published 2016 in Romanian in Romania), *The Forbidden City on Water* (Translated into Russian and published in 2021 by Avant-garde Press in Moscow, co-translated by Zhang Bing, Wu Ping and Alekce Filimonov, *The Speed of Sadness* (published November 2019 in Korean in Korea), *Seeds of Job's Tears*, translated by Wolfgang Kubin and published in Austria in 2021 and others.

Her work has been translated into German, English, Japanese, Korean, Vietnamese, Persian, Arabic, Bengali and Spanish. Her paintings have been exhibited in 'An Art Exhibition for Contemporary Chinese Poets' and 'A Show of Calligraphy and Paintings for Contemporary Chinese Men and Women of Letters'. Her long poem, 'Sad Songs from another World', is regarded as one of the most representative works for women's literature in the 1990s and, when translated by Ouyang Yu into English, was published as the title piece in *Long Poem Magazine* in the U.K. She was invited to do a reading at the launch of *Long Poem Magazine* in Barbican Centre in London.

Xiao Xiao has won numerous poetry awards in China and overseas, such as the Wen Yiduo Poetry Award, the Special Contribution Award for a Century of New Poetry, the Annual Poetry Award by *Poetry Tide* magazine, the Poetry Award by *Beijing Literature* magazine, the First Award for the ten top poems in 2017 by China Poetry Net, one of the top ten poets in 2018, and the Tudor Arghezi international poetry prize in 2016 in Romania, of which she is the first Asian recipient. She has also been awarded the title of Honorary Citzen of Targu Carbunesti in Romania in 2016. In 2020, the entry under 'Xiao Xiao', written by Wolfgang Kubin, was included in the largest literary dictionary in Germany and also in Europe, *Kritisches Lexikon für fremdsprachige Gegenwartsliteratur* (KLfG digital).

99.9 平方

我的爱正好99.9平方
可以安放一张会隐身术的床
和一间白纸黑字的书房

开放的客厅
私通荡漾的大海
几朵耍性子的云在天花上悲伤

我的爱小于一个妻子
是爱的圆周率的 N 次方
是肉肉，是心肝偶尔的小刺痛

连你责怪、批评的语调
也是宽阔、和善而性感的
让我有些耍赖，着迷

有一天
如果你爱不动了
那一定是我的99.9平方
越来越小

不是你的错

（2017 年 12 月 30 日）

99.9 Square

My love is exactly 99.9 square
that can fit a bed, capable of invisible tricks
and a study, of white paper and black words

an open guestroom
in private intercourse with a rippling sea
wilful clouds, saddening on the sky-flowers

my love is smaller than a wife
as it is to the nth degree of the circumference ratio of love
it's flesh-flesh, the occasional little piercing pain of heart

even your chiding and criticizing tone
is broad, amiable and sexy
that makes me make a scene, captivating me

one day
when you can't love any more
it'll be because my 99.9 square
is getting smaller

not your fault

有时，一个词

秋天，通过黄金的十月
嚼着舌头，叫来
一杯杯烈性的二锅头

眼看着一首诗的光芒缩进肉体
把人心弄得飞起来

有人在一口气中出走
有人在一个句子中悔恨
有人在借一些词语杀人

一场暴雨像耳光落了下来
秋天，这黄金的软有些招架不住

有人借着酒劲用假象来支撑，却忘了
有时一个词可以要你飞到天上
也可以要你生不如死

（2009年10月27日晨5点）

Sometimes, a Word

In the autumn, you, chewing the tongue
called for a fiery Erguotuo, one cup after another
through the golden October

while watching the ray of a poem withdraw into the body
setting the heart a-wing

someone ran away, with a breath of anger
someone regretted, in a sentence
and someone else killed, by borrowing a number of words

a storm fell, like a slap across the face
in the autumn, the softness of gold was hard to stand

someone propped himself up on the strength of liquor but he forgot
that while a word could get you to fly skyward
it could also get you to live a death-like life

痛和一缕死亡的青烟

这些年，我一直在酸楚
这朵空空的云中
最喜欢的人，在气候外变冷
在命运里挣扎
一夜之间，被内心的大风吹到了天涯

坏消息像一场暴雨越下越大
我撑着伞，雨在空中突然停止
记忆的疼痛从半空瓢泼
我浑身发抖，无处可去

一场春天的鹅毛大雪，短暂而诡秘
世界变态，浮在冰凉的水面
我悄悄流泪，雨雪
又在我的脸上下起来

伸手触摸，痛和一缕死亡的青烟
从指尖爬上额头
秋天的死皮在冬天的脸上削落
爱，一步跨进了冬天
我用疼到骨髓的伤口斟酒
一生一世，嫁给了空气

（2006-4-25凌晨4点，2006-11-16抄改）

Pain and a Wisp of Blue Smoke of Death

Over the years, I have been feeling quite depressed
in this hollow and empty cloud
the one I love best is growing cold outside the climate
struggling in the fate
and blown, in a big wind, to the end of the earth overnight

bad news, like a storm, rains harder and harder
when I hold up my umbrella, the rain stops in the air, abruptly
pain of memory pours, from mid-air
I tremble all over, nowhere to go

a big snow, like goose feathers, in spring, is short and surreptitious
the world is morbid, floating on the icy-cold water
quietly, I am shedding tears when rain and snow
fall, again, on my face

when I touch with my hand, pain and a wisp of blue smoke of death
creeps from my fingertips to my forehead
the dead skin of the autumn is peeling off of the winter's face
love, in one step, strides into winter
with the wound painful to the bone-marrow, I hold liquor
and I'm married to the air, for the rest of my life

灵魂树下

既然生必须接受死这个母亲
日暮后，一个人提着光阴的口袋
捡拾灵魂树下垂落的果子
死之核，攥在颤抖的手中
伤痛的籽粒，一颗一颗饱满

呼吸爱因斯坦的风
从彼岸吹来，搜刮全身
掩埋寒冷和腐朽
用血与骨髓，心与腹
用生来延续死，用死来延续生

其实没有胜算，风伸出舌头
它舔到尸群新鲜的味道
把瞬间无度的死，撒上盐，撒上时间
焚烧，不停息吹向灰烬的空白
吹向更远

（2008年11月21日夜）

Under the Tree of Soul

Now that life must accept this death, a Mother
someone carries a bag of time, after sundown
and picks up the fruit that has dropped under the tree of soul
the kernel of death, tightly grasped in his trembling hand
and seeds of wound, full seeds

Einstein's wind, being breathed in
is blowing from the other shore, raking and scraping one's whole person
with blood and bone-marrow, heart and belly
to continue death with life and to continue life with death

while in fact there is no winning, the wind sticks out its tongue
licking the fresh taste of the corpses
sprinkling the instant, degree-less death with salt, with time
burning, and ceaselessly blowing into the ashen blanks
blowing further

我愿意赔罪

这个二月
我摸着父亲的额头
看着他
从13楼的病床
去了另一个世界

守灵、烧纸
温坟、头七
我一直念叨父亲
顺着光走，抵达彼岸

人间有太多的
伤、别、悲、痛
黑、暗、苦、难

父亲走后的"二七"
他生活多年的温江
七中实验中学
让春天迷乱
让真相在人间变形

有人将姜黄粉、红曲米
撒在鸡腿上
制造魔幻视频
有人对家长
用辣椒水
做最低限度的警械

老师说：
"生霉是生霉了

I'd Love to Apologize

Last February
I touched Father's forehead
watching him go to the other world
from his sick bed on the 13th floor

keeping vigil, burning the papers
to warm up the grave and to observe the first 7th Day
I was thinking of Father
of how he went along the light till he reached the other shore

there was too much
wounding, departure, sadness, pain
darkness, gloom, bitterness, misery

on the second 7th Day after Father's departure
No. 7 Middle School, an experimental school
at Wenjiang, where he lived many years
called the spring to be confused
and the truth to be twisted in the world

as there were people who had sprinkled the chicken legs
with Turmeric powder and red yeast rice
in producing magic video clips
and there were people who used pepper water
as a warning, at the lowest limit

the teacher said:
'it's mouldy, for sure
but we'll have to check to see
if it endangers health'

危不危害健康
还要查了才知道"

我愤怒、绝望
在喉咙里诅咒
腐败的鱿鱼、牛肉
变质的调料、瓜果
糯米烧麦

孩子们便秘
口腔溃疡、胃痛、恶心
成了谎言
媒体数据：
905名学生就诊
无明显异常

我脑洞大开
现实与虚构
都像真的

哦，天上的父亲
看见了吗
真相让一些人那么恐惧
我愿意低下头颅
向遮掩的禁忌
向汹涌的沉默
赔罪

（2019年3月21日晨6：34；2019年4月26日修改）

I was angry and I was in despair
cursing in my throat
the decaying squid and beef
the spoiled ingredients, melons and fruit
and the Shumai, of glutinous rice

that kids are now constipated
they suffer from mouth ulcer, stomach-ache and nausea
has been made into a lie
as the media have the statistics:
when 905 students went for consultation
there's no obvious abnormality

my brain-hole now wide open
as both reality and virtuality
seemed real

well, Father in heaven
did you see that
truth made people so fearful?
I'm willing to lower my head
to apologize
to the covered-up taboos
and the surging silences

移交

深秋，露出满嘴假牙
像一个黄昏的老人
在镜中假眠

他暗地里
把一连串的错误与后悔
移交给冬天

把迟钝的耳朵和过敏的鼻子
移交给医学
把缺心少肺的时代
移交给诗歌

把过去的阴影和磨难
移交给伤痕
把破碎的生活
移交给我

记忆，一些思想的皮屑
落了下来
这钻石中深藏的影子
像光阴漏尽的小虫

密密麻麻的，死亡
是一堂必修课
早晚会来敲门

Transference

Deep autumn, revealing a mouthful of dentures
was taking a nap, in the mirror
like an old man in the evening

in private, he
transferred a series of errors
and regrets to winter

handing the slow ears and sensitive noses
over to medicine
and handing the age lacking in hearts
over to poetry

handing the shadows and suffering of the past
over to wounds
handing a fragmented life
over to me

memory, with a few furfurs of thinking
has fallen
this shadow, hidden deep inside the diamond
resembles the gnats whose time has all leaked through

dense, death
is a compulsory course
as it will come and knock on the door, sooner or later

深秋，这铁了心的老人
从镜中醒来，握着
死的把柄
将收割谁的皮肤和头颅

（2014年）

deep autumn, the old man whose heart is steeled
wakes up in the mirror, handling
the handle of death
no one knows whose skin or head he's going to harvest

抱紧江南

江南的秋，
好多小昆虫叫哥哥，
爱熟透了……
伸着懒腰的花瓣
被雨点、蝈蝈叫开，
迎面流淌的颜色，
命令孤独与死亡的风景，
卷起一湖山水。

那些吹进骨缝的
痒酥酥的粉，
细碎的欲望，
迎着晨曦的光亮，
还有些湿润。
那个烟花女子
用突破局限的果实，
用死，喂养传统的后人。
她的汹涌？
她与黑暗的拥抱？
只有熟透的爱能隐忍……

熟透的爱……
如沉香进入她命运的弱点
她生前死了两次，
死后被掘墓，
又死了一次。
她的前世今生都嫁给了悲剧。

虞山锦峰下的旧坟，
比想象更缭乱，荒凉。

Holding River South in a Tight Hug

Autumn in River South
so many insects are calling out: Ge Ge (Bro)
love, thoroughly ripe...
petals, stretching themselves
to open, in response to the raindrops, the chirping of the grasshoppers
colours, flowing right into one's face
were ordering solitude and the landscape of death
to roll up a lakeful of mountains and waters

the itchy powders
blown into the crack of the bones
the fragmentary desire
facing the light of dawn
a bit wet
the smoke-flower woman
fed the offspring of tradition
with fruit that broke out of the limitations, and with death
her turbulence?
her embrace with the darkness?
only thoroughly ripe love can endure...

thoroughly ripe love...
like agarwood, entered into the weakness of her fate
she had died twice before she died
when her grave was dug up
she died again
her previous life and her present life were both married to tragedy

an old grave at the foot of Jinfeng in Yushan
was more messy and desolate than imagination

打结的茅草低着头，
像寻找葬进泥土的秘密
夜里，犀利的风
再一次冒犯入土的灵魂
这枯草败叶中开出的野花，
无遮无拦……

而那些肌肤、香料、
灯草、骨头与旧瓷，
穿过生死的密纹
倚靠一张乌镇的雕花木桌
来摆放记忆。
抖落疲惫、愤怒、焦虑、
无奈、暴力、哀悼……
一切逼近负面的词……

用黄酒洗心革面，
用梅子解开姜丝，
抱紧江南的秋色，
抱紧刚刚落下枝头的告别，
抱紧身体里
最危险的一滴晕眩
抱紧落日，
那粉身碎骨的一声喊
抱紧重逢死亡的一首诗……

正如错开死亡的富春山居图，
逃出一团团殉葬的火焰，
用古典、歉意的美
让后现代弯腰，
纸上残留的风景，
如罪孽般温柔。

（2014 年）

where the entangled couch grasses were hanging their heads
as if in search of the secrets buried in the mud
at night, the piercing wind
once again violated the soul that had been interred
the wild flowers that sprouted out of the withered grasses and fallen leaves
without hindrance...

and those skins, spices
lamp grasses, bones and old china
went through the dense veins of life and death
relying on a carved table of Wuzhen
for the placement of memory
getting rid of fatigue, fury, anxiety
helplessness, violence, mourning...
all the words closing in on the negative...

washing the heart with yellow rice wine
loosening the shredded ginger with plums
holding tight the colours of autumn in River South
holding tight the farewell that has just dropped out of a branch
holding tight the most dangerous drop of dizziness
inside the body
holding tight the setting sun
the cry that shattered the bones
and holding tight the poem that meets death again...

just like the painting, 'The Fuchun Mountain Residence' that sets death aside
from which flames of a funeral escape
with classic, apologetic beauty
that causes the postmodern to bend at the waist
the landscape that remains on the paper
as tender as sin

平民列传

北京甄婶

一、
99 岁的甄婶
一天到晚出出进进
扭得扭得
院里院外十几趟

你不知道她要干什么
她也不知道
只有十一点的时候，她说
开始给儿子准备午饭了

马上要拆迁的四月的院子
过道上落满了
不知哪来的枯叶
垮塌的小屋废墟
长出了绿草

她像往常一样
看看那些搬得走
和搬不走的东西
搬不走的是
刻在青灰砖上的目光
能搬走的是那些记忆
她不知道那些记忆能搬走多远
因为明年她就 100 岁了

Biographies of the Ordinary People: A Sequence

Aunty Zhen in Beijing

1.
Aunty Zhen, at 99
goes in and out, of the courtyard
day in and day out
gingerly

you do not know what she wants to do
she doesn't know herself
it's not till 11 a.m. that she said
she's going to prepare lunch for her son

the courtyard, due for demolition soon in April
has a pathway covered
with fallen leaves from nowhere
and from the ruins of a collapsed hut
green grass grows

like before
she takes a look at the movables
and things that refuse to be moved
which are
the eyes on the steel-grey bricks
whereas the movables are the memories
she has no idea how far the memories can be moved
because she'll turn 100 next year

二、

孤独不是一个人的瞎想
是她一个人来回的溜达

年轻时的她唱过青衣
人和一个院落的离别
就是一出戏

墙角儿那口咸菜缸
年年都在她手下出来滋味
她青筋暴露的手
胡鲁着缸沿儿
一只蜘蛛胡鲁到空荡荡的缸里

该走了，儿子的车
停在院门口
甄婶说：我要那口腌菜缸
儿子说：不要
"不要吗？"
"不要！"
甄婶过去
从窗台上搬起压菜石
砸向菜缸，扭头就走
她走着，踩踏着
破碎的呻吟

三、

明年甄婶就100岁了

（2019年4月17日）

2.

Loneliness is not the wild thoughts of one person
it's her strollings, to and fro, all by herself

she played the role of a Black Cloth[1] when young
a woman and her departure from her courtyard
were a play on its own

in the corner, there was a vat of pickles
year in and year out, taste would grow, from under her hands
her hands with exposed blue veins
touching the edge of the vat
flipping a spider into the hollow vat

it's time to go as her son's car
was parked outside the entrance
Aunty Zhen said, 'I want that pickles vat'
Her son said, 'No'
'No?'
'No!'
Aunty Zhen went over
picked up a stone, for pressing the pickles, from the windowsill
and smashed the vat, before she turned to go
she walked, treading
the broken moanings

3.

Next year, Aunty Zhen will turn 100

---

1 Pronounced 'qingyi', a role reserved for women, young and old, in Ping Opera.

枫丹白露驼背人

一、

枫丹白露小区的锅炉工
是个罗锅
多年前烧煤的时代
也有人叫他煤黑子
黑的脸
黑的衣服
黑的鞋
沾满煤灰

黎明，他走出锅炉房
走进阳光灿烂的街区
就像残存的一坨黑夜

如今，岁月更替
整洁的工装
清静的环境
却是命运弄人
他难以入眠
蹑手蹑脚出去散步
怕惊落树上成熟的果子
怕惊醒楼群里熟睡的灯光

二、

门房问：驼大哥
我总这么叫你不好吧
他答：驼就是罗锅
有什么不好

The Hunchbacked Man at Fontainebleau

1.

The boiler at Fontainebleau Neighbourhood
is Luoguo (hunchbacked)
many years, in the age of coal-burning
people called him Black Coal
a black face
black clothes
black shoes
covered with coal dust

at dawn, when he walks out of the boiler room
into the sunny block
like a remaining heap of dark night

now, years after
clean uniform
quiet environment
but, because of the playful fate
he finds it hard to fall asleep
so he tiptoes out for a walk
afraid of surprising the fruit so they fall
afraid of waking up the lights asleep in the crowd of the buildings

2.

The janitor said: Brother Hunchback
that's no good, isn't it?
he said: Hunchback is Luoguo
what is bad about it?

罗锅欠着身子
头比一般人更低
更老实
我就想做个老实人
叫什么都行

三、

某一天，门房高喊
"驼大哥，有客人找，
女的"
他冲出锅炉房乐了
张开双臂拥抱着行李
二人进屋，房门紧闭
门房拍拍脑壳
自言自语：
哦，又是一个驼背

（2019 年 4 月 17）

a Luoguo is bent double
whose head is lower than others
he's more honest
all I want to be is an honest person
whatever you call me

3.

One day, the janitor cried out loud
'Brother Hunchback, someone is looking for you
a woman'
when he rushed out of the boiler room, he was delighted
his arms spread open, he hugged the luggage
the two of them went in, with the door shut
the janitor, patting himself on the head
said to himself:
oh, another hunchback!

过街桥上的无名诗人

一、

十二月的过街桥
在北京数不清
这座过街桥
桥头有座华堂
桥上一个人在兜售
蜷缩瑟瑟
矮小身子
却眉飞色舞

寒风抖动
翻开
他手里的书页
他的心思
他的脑筋
他的牛逼哄哄

《无名的过街桥》
让我停下了
无名的脚步
一本诗集100块

二、

问他：住在哪里
答：居无定所
问：吃呢
答：卖了书有馒头吃
卖不出饿肚子

An Unknown Poet on the Overpass

1.

There are countless overpasses
in December, in Beijing
this one
has a gorgeous hall at its head
someone is selling something
curling up
a short guy
but he is beaming with joy

the cold wind is shivering
turning
the pages in his hand
his heart-thoughts
his brain
his top of the rangeness

The Unknown Overpass
caused me to stop
in my unknown tracks
his poetry, priced at 100 bucks a copy

2.

I asked him: Where do you live
He said: No fixed residence
I asked: Where do you find your food?
He said: If I sell a copy, I've got steamed bread
        or I starve

问：为什么单选这座过街桥
答：昨天我住昌平
坐441换558再596
此处离下车点最近

我买了两本，问：
你知道或熟悉哪些诗人
他说：不知道，也不熟悉
他们与我有什么关系
他们与我写诗有什么关系
就像桥下来来往往的车
与我和过街桥有什么关系
但我知道
你应该是一个诗人

我等待他下面的询问
他的目光却打了折扣
转向几个凑过来的女孩

穿红衣服的女孩惊叹：
哇，这么贵
系蓝围巾的女孩体恤：
写这么一大本不容易
梳小辫的女孩噘着嘴：
好，也是好！
贵，还是贵！

他拍着书说
这是馒头，这是食粮
这是精神食粮
蓝围巾的女孩摇着头
掏出钱来

I asked: Why on this overpass?
He said: I stayed in Changping yesterday
        I took 441, changed for 558, then 596
        it's closest to the bus-stop

I bought two copies and asked:
do you know any poets or are you familiar with any
he said: don't know, not familiar
what have they got to do with me
just like the cars coming and going underneath the overpass
they have nothing to do with either me or the overpass
but as far as I know
you ought to be a poet

I waited for more of his questions
but his eyes, at a discount
were directed towards the girls crowding over

the one in red expressed her surprise:
wow, so expensive!
the one with a blue shawl was more understanding:
it's not easy to produce such a big book
the one with a little piggy tail pursed her lips:
good, that's good!
expensive, that's expensive!

he patted his book and said
this is steamed bread and this is food
this is spiritual food
the girl in blue shawl shook her head
as she brought out the money

这个结果让我抱着两本书
走过了过街桥

三、

在桥下
我继续关注着他
来来往往的人
匆匆而过

我在想
诗人啊诗人
你没有必要
也不应该
长时间停留在一个地方
也可以走过过街桥
到这边来试一试

（2019年4月17日）

it was this result that let me hug the two copies
as I walked across the overpass

3.

Underneath the overpass
I kept paying attention to him
but people coming and going
hurried over

I was thinking to myself
Poet, oh, poet
it's not necessary for you
to stay in one place for long
nor should you do so
you might like walk across the overpass
and give it a go on this side

未知

十月给我一束危险的光
我对着飘落的树叶
发呆

不敢触摸深秋的古琴

酸涩的旋律
像长在心里的山楂
一颗颗从眼角滚落

此刻素未谋面的人
在路上，是谁
是我命中的哪一个

是否也感到嘴里微苦
有一滴泪从眼前飞过

此刻，你如说嫁
我就允诺

此刻，你如说到某个黑夜
我就像命运的星星
低垂下来

（2017年10月1日夜）

The Unknown

October gave me a bunch of dangerous lights
I, dazed
faced a falling leaf

daring not to touch the ancient zither, deep in the autumn

the sour rhythms
like the hawthorns, growing in my heart
teardrops falling out of the corners of my eyes

the person I haven't so far met
is on his way, who is he
which one is it in my fate

does he also feel the slight bitterness in the mouth
also a drop of tear flying across the eye

right now, if you say marry
I'll do

right now, if you mention a certain night
I'll lower myself
like a star of fate

今生遇见

我的小宇宙已被你打开
隐瞒在世俗里的星辰都在发光
涌向那条秘密的通道
奔向你

那些带电的数字与字母
那些着火的词语
今生遇见，会烧伤自己

你要退到三里以外数星星
然后隔岸观火么
我触碰到你向左的呼吸
慢慢冷却下来

那些我们之间发生的前朝旧事
会在一次打碎的诺言中
再次风生水起

（2011年1月25日早晨）

Meeting This Life

My little universe having been opened by you
all the stars, hidden in the secular world, are now lit
surging towards the secret path
rushing towards you

the charged numbers and letters
the words set alight
they'll scorch myself if I meet them this life

you must beat a retreat and count the stars three *li* beyond here
then watch the fire burning from the other side
when I hit your breath going left
I'll grow gradually cold

things of a previous dynasty that happened between us
will rise up like wind
in a broken promise

那一夜

那一夜，躲着寒风
我走了一生的弯路，来到你的面前
你用一杯清水，让我坐下，抖落前尘
然后，端出一杯绿茶的距离
坐在我的左侧

你越来越紧张、慌乱
偷偷地深呼吸
在一句话的半途停了停
突然抓住我的手说：
"心里早就有鬼，跳得好快"

我摸着你满怀小鹿的秘密
才明白
半世情缘悬在心尖
桃花为你在我脸上误入歧途

你用了两年的克制来等待
而此时，导火索被你一点燃，我就爆炸了

（2011年元月26日深夜）

That Night

That night, hiding myself from the cold wind
I walked a lifetime of circuitous road to come up to you
with a glass of clean water, you sat me down and shook off the dust of a
                                                                    previous life
then, you produced the distance of a cup of green tea
sat on my left side

you got more and more tense, and panicked
stealing deep breaths
and pausing half way in a sentence
then, all of a sudden, you grabbed hold of my hand and said:
'you've got a devil in your heart as it's beating so fast'

touching your secret, pregnant with a little deer
I became aware
a half lifetime of love was hanging on the tip of heart
the peach flowers, for you, got astray on my face

it had taken you a two-year restraint to wait
but now, I exploded once my fuse was ignited

今晚芒果会失眠

到了柳州
与我相逢的第一棵
果树是那么低矮
我克制不住自己的右手
去触摸树上的
两只芒果
是那么的性感、柔滑
像大自然的一对
青涩的小乳房
你摸它
它会害羞地颤栗
今晚芒果会失眠了

（2015年6月9日）

The Mango Would be Sleepless Tonight

When I arrived in Liuzhou
the first fruit tree that met me
was so low
I couldn't help reaching to touch
the two mangoes on the tree
with my own right hand
as they were so sexy, so smooth
like a pair of green breasts
in nature
when you touched them
they would become shy and shiver
the mangoes would be sleepless tonight

一个外省的女子

这个外省的女子，突然
来到北方的心脏失眠
没有碰到雪片结实的肉体
这个冬天，这个永不到达的英雄
生活在别处
她的沮丧，她的隐秘
她庞大的城堡——此处空候

像一个愤世忧伤的情人
深入夜，撕开更黑的
伏在风中，穿透南方的胸脯
她敏感的头巾和手套
兴奋地吃掉流下的眼泪
她的脸滑向一片空地
空空的，只有士兵吞噬着氧气

这个外省的女子惊动了谁
听，广场下面的声音
无数的脸歪着，喘着粗气
在闲言碎语的空壳中生锈

逃到别处的冬天
她记忆中的另一场血，生动地活着
冷却的嘴唇长满了铜剑
她昏厥的手招摇着
一只呼啸的乌鸦再一次
把死亡和危险放在心上

A Woman from the Provinces

This woman, from the provinces, suddenly
Came to the north, with her solid body, of an insomniac heart
And that had not touched snow-flakes
This winter, that hero never reachable
Is elsewhere
Her dejection, her secrecy
And her huge castle: waiting here for nothing

She, like a cynical lover
Penetrated the night, tearing open the darker
Prostrate in the wind, going through the breast of the south
With her sensitive scarf and gloves
Eating the shed tears, excitedly
Her face slipping to an empty land
Empty, where only the soldiers were devouring the oxygen

The woman from the provinces must have disturbed someone
Listen: the noise from below the Square
Countless faces aslant, breathing heavily
Rusting in the shell of broken words

Escaped to a winter elsewhere
Another bloodshed in her memory, vividly alive
A fill of bronze swords on her cold lips
Her fainted hands waving
A screaming magpie, once again
Placed death and danger over the heart

唯有灵魂一无所有

越来越多的苦难开口
越来越多的谎言面如桃花，插满了耳朵
越来越多的假象从眼睛张开翅膀
越来越多的腐朽掐住黑暗的咽喉

越来越多的丑陋从肺腑，落井下石
越来越多的时尚在轻浮的罪孽中枝叶繁茂
越来越多的金币收割着神经的末梢
越来越多的苦果含在嘴里交给悔恨

越来越多的阴影在胸前十面埋伏
越来越多的栋梁扭曲成微笑的麻木
越来越多的罪行滋润骨质疏松的黑手
越来越多的恶之花结果烂熳的毒瘤

越来越多的疼痛钻进每一个人的皮肉与骨血
越来越多的病毒增加着死亡的重量
唯有灵魂越来越轻，越来越轻
入肉

The Soul is the Only Thing that does not Possess Anything

More and more suffering is opening its mouth
More and more lies, with peach-flower faces, have grown ears
More and more falsehood is sticking its wings out of the eyes
More and more corruption is seizing the darkness by the throat

More and more ugliness is rubbing salt into the wound in the lungs
More and more fashion is flourishing in the flirting sins
More and more money is reaping the nerve endings
More and more bitter fruit, in the mouth, is handed over to regrets

More and more shadows are lying in ambush all round, on the chest
More and more pillars of state are twisted into numb smiles
More and more crime are nourishing the osteoporosis of black hands
More and more fleurs du mal end up in brilliant tumors of poison

More and more pain is creeping into the bones and blood
More and more viruses are adding to the weight of death
Except the soul becoming lighter and lighter
That is entering into the flesh

打碎的死，舞蹈
——为我临摹的画配诗

冬天的脚趾已渐渐靠近房门
在外面的冷，突然如此暴虐
袭击了我全身

室内，空气颓丧
菊花凄楚地叹息
在哪里？我跌倒
摔破了眉骨和手臂

这挑剔的暴力，跨越记忆
扑进我怀中
连疼痛都变得麻木

玉镯流着血，阴影冲进卧室
碎片拿走了我心上的生命
哦，黄金的动作，美的极端
在纸上围着圆圈，手拉手

打碎的死，肉体
飞落的绝色舞蹈
都是我相亲相爱的邻居

Death Smashed, Dancing

Winter's toes, gradually, are drawing nigh to the door
The coldness, outside, is turning suddenly violent
Attacking me throughout my person

Inside, the air, listless
The chrysanthemum sighing a sad sigh
Where? I fall
Breaking my brow-bones and my arms

This picky violence, stepping across memory
Throws itself into my arms
Rendering even pain numb

The jade bracelet bleeding, the shadow rushing into my bedroom
Broken pieces removing the life from my heart
Humph, the act of gold, the extreme of beauty
Making a ring, on the paper, hand in hand

Death smashed, the flesh
Peerlessly beautiful dance, that flies and falls
All my loved neighbours

一支黄鹤楼

有时，一个人比一棵
掉光了叶子的树，
还要孤独
与树木相比
那些经历过的大事小事
都变成了枯枝
随意、自在、慵懒地
留在生活里晃动
风一吹，堆积的负担
就簌簌落了下来

有时，人生也要退一步
抿一口胎菊茶、荷叶水
弯曲一下生锈的手指
挪动一下命运中的黑
似乎，一种诱惑开始上升
卡在嗓子眼，迫不及待
来，点燃一支黄鹤楼
深吸一口，吐纳
再深吸一口，慢慢吐出
就像吐出那些
在内心汹涌起来的孤独

A Yellow Crane Tower

Sometimes, one is more lonely
than a tree
that has shed all its leaves
compared with a tree
all those things, big and small, that have been experienced
have turned into withered twigs
random, leisurely and lazy
wobbling in life
with the blowing of a wind, the heaped burdens
fall, soughing

Sometimes, one has to retreat backwards
taking a sip of baby chrysanthemum tea, and lotus-leave water
bending one's rusty fingers
as one moves the darkness in one's fate
as if a temptation is beginning to rise
stuck, as it is, in the throat, getting impatient
Come, light up a Yellow Crane Tower
take a deep drag before breathing it out
another deep drag, before letting it out, slowly
like breathing out
those solitudes surging, in the heart of hearts

耳鸣的花朵

今夜，睡眠又一次把我推出门外
时间的鸦片在春天的肌肤上冒着黑烟
烧烤着我2007年4月凌晨3点40分的心
紧张的烟尘飘落在脸上慢慢变灰
我坐在失眠的板凳上出神

草丛越长越高，从去年的杂乱中
藏满了虫鸣，朝我深夜的耳朵蜂拥而至
捂着灵魂的手怎么也不听使唤
你的心跳，连同整个夜晚发呆的星星
在不确定的深处，隐藏着我绝望的惊喜

为忧伤脱落的头发向生活的边缘
纷乱飞扬起来
在边陲的黄昏，突然有人感到寒冷
春天在一瞬间被拴在了北冰洋上

花朵忍着痛贴近你
氧气不够用爱来呼吸
从未改变，在心中，在永远
我宁愿死，干干净净地
用一生来拽紧耳鸣的岁月
用另一生来追赶梦想的花朵

Flowers of Tinnitus

Tonight, sleep has again pushed me outdoors
The opium of time sends up black smokes from the skin of spring
Burning my heart at 3.40am, in April, 2007
Tense ashes, fluttering down on the face, turn slowly grey
I, entranced, am sitting on an insomniac stool

The cluster of grass is growing higher and higher, from last year's mess
Hidden with the insects' noise, crowding into my late night ears
My hand, covering my soul, refuses to be womanned
The leap of your heart, along with the dazed stars of all night
In the depth of uncertainties, is hidden my delight in despair

Hair, shed for sorrow, is flying in chaos
Towards the edge of life
At dusk, in a borderland, someone suddenly feels the cold
The spring, for an instant, becomes latched on to the Arctic Ocean

The flowers, bearing the pain, get close to you
There is not sufficient oxygen for love to breathe
Never changing, in the heart, never for ever
I'd rather die, cleanly
Holding fast to the years of tinnitus, with my whole life
And chasing the flowers of dream, in another life

十月在牙缝里被咬碎

十月在牙缝里被咬碎
秋天解开欺骗的腰带变得辛辣绝情
至今，那些留下的硬伤
流着鲜血，流着卑微、流着死缓

气在喉咙一点一点下沉
身体越来越轻
心、肝、肉、头发、指甲
都不能自己

在失控中等待一场被迫的革命
命运挥着世态炎凉的皮鞭
抽打牙缝里的十月
抽打我精疲力竭的灵魂

接近五年，扳着指头，掐着光阴
用无限的想象取代了烤焦的现实
不可言传的滋味迅速到了极限
使那些高大的形象和灿烂的日子
变得渺小而潮湿

十月，十月，在这里出生
注定拐弯的我，绕道而行
十月，十月，一个夜晚的小动作
撕开真相，消灭了我抒情的一生

October Squashed between My Teeth

October squashed between my teeth
Autumn, after loosening its girdle, becomes poignant, relentless
Even till today, the hard injuries that remain
Are still flowing with blood, with low status, with something short of death

The air, little by little, is sinking in my throat
My body is getting lighter
My heart, my liver, my flesh, my hair and my finger-nails
None of them able to control themselves

Waiting for a forced revolution that has lost control
Fate is brandishing a whip of cynicism
To lash at the October in my teeth
And at my spent soul

Close to five years now, I count it on my fingers, against the time
Replacing the scorched realities with limitless imagination
The taste, too much for words, is so fast it reaches the limit
Belittling the image, high and mighty, and the days of brilliance
And making them wet

October, October, that's where I am born
Destined to make a turn, I make a detour
October, October, a small act one night
Has torn down the true image, destroying my lyrical life

被灵魂追赶的人

我被灵魂追赶
飞得越远，越高
越无处可逃
转过身
一滴花露碰碎刀尖
下雨了

废气包裹的楼群
与云朵擦肩而过
我累了，踩着刀锋
朝贬低的生活迈了一步

把苦难扔进炉火，用孤独温酒
像企鹅练习飞一样，摔倒
在疼痛与无奈的细节中
接受一场命运的大雪

欲望，奔向今世
道德迎风瓦解，人间乱了方寸
我被浮尘撞倒，一颗灵魂
再一次挂在刀尖上
使每一个夜晚意外地尖锐
每一个清晨锋利无比

Someone Chased by the Soul

Chased by my soul, the farther
And higher I flew
The fewer places I could run to
The second I turned back
A drop of flower dew touched the point of a knife and broke
It began raining

The crowd of buildings, wrapped up in a smog of waste airs
Scraped their shoulders with the clouds
Tired, I, treading knife-blades
Stepped towards the reduced life

Chuck the misery into the fire and warm the wine with solitude
Fall, like a penguin
Accept a huge snow of fate
In the detail of pain and helplessness

Desires, rushing into this world
Morality collapsing, with the wind, and the world, in turmoil
I was fetched down by the floating dust, a soul
Again hanging from the point of the knife
Making every night unexpectedly sharp
And every morning incredibly incisive

冬　天

这个冬天宁静而傲慢
这个冬天和冰雪降落在高处
好白，好白啊
我站在风口，心在上升
纯净的灵魂！雪
这个高处的奇迹

我是否认错了天气
积雪的树上长满了梨子
和往日一样甘美，清香
许多事物欣喜若狂
感谢此时活着或者死
多么偶然又刻骨的幸福
在雪白的边缘
我一身的花瓣骤然消失

Winter

This winter, still and aloof
All the ice and snow have fallen on higher places
So white, and, oh, such whiteness
I was standing at the mouth of the wind, my heart ascending
A pure soul! The snow
A miracle at this higher place

Did I wrongly recognize the weather
That I saw the snowed trees filled with pears
As sweet and fragrant as olden days
So many things so happy
Thanking the moment for being alive or dead?
What incidental and bone-carving happiness!
At the edge of snow-whiteness
The petals, covering me up, suddenly vanished

等候

秋天很深了
瓦砾上淫雨霏霏
当种子返回泥土，被凭空的气候
消灭在不露痕迹之中
这样的意外，一个女人
在空空的瓶子中升起
平静地流泪，度过死

一个下午，我在菊花的气息中
等候某一张脸缓缓落下
也许我猛然老丑
收拾起阳台上艳丽的衣衫
而你，一个书信中的过客
遥遥无期，身世悲壮
暴露的危险何时抵达边缘

一只隐藏的飞禽是否死于猝然的早雪
它的羽毛是否比雪还要温暖
但冬天到来，我只能用一首诗等你
当迷乱的菊花洁白，飞满了蝴蝶
幸福就会悄然降临

Waiting

The autumn deepening
Excessive rain on the debris
As the seeds returned to the soil, the climate of sheer fabrication
Was exterminated in the tracelessness
Such an unexpectedness, a woman
Rose in an empty bottle
Shedding tears quietly, spending death

One afternoon, I, in the smell of chrysanthemum
Was waiting for a face to fall slowly
Perhaps, I'd grow old and ugly, on a sudden
As I put away the pretty clothes on the balcony
And you, a transient guest in a letter
At a far distant future time, with a tragically moving life
When would you arrive at the brink of exposed danger?

Would a hidden flying fowl die in an abrupt early snow?
Would its feathers be warmer than the snow?
However, when the winter came, all I could do is wait for you with a poem
When the confused chrysanthemum whitened, filled with flying butterflies
Happiness would quietly descend

多年以后

日子一天一天在流水中
打着水漂
有些约定本生就是泡影
有些爱注定用来辜负
用来转身

多年后，我头发花白
牙齿脱落
开满波斯菊的皱褶脸上
唯有眼睛依然透明

我独自一人，佩戴爱的首饰
怀着一颗转世的心
带着仓央嘉措的诗篇
登上开往布达拉宫的火车

某一天，在那个传说的
拉萨小酒馆里
一个角落，坐着放下的我
海拔高处，夜晚打开
一瓶青稞酒

酥油灯的火苗
映在我淡定、平和的额头上
折射出岁月的坎坷
而我饱满的情绪回到
从前的那一个夜晚

也许我等待着一个人的来临
也许，也许，只为了仅仅
仅仅与一个灵魂对饮

Many Years After

Days in the flow of waters
Like ducks and drakes being played
Some dates themselves bubbles
Some love, fated to fail
To turn around

Many years after, I, white-haired
Teeth fallen
A face filled with garden cosmos
Except the eyes, still lucid

I, alone, wearing the jewelry of love
And a reincarnated heart
Carrying poems by Sangs-Ryyas Rgyamtsho
On board a train to the Potala

One day, in a corner of that
Legendary restaurant
In Lhasa, I, the one who let go
As the night approached, opened a bottle
Of qingke barley wine from the plateau

The flame in the yak butter lamp
Reflected on my calm and peaceful forehead
Refracting the ups and downs of the years
As my full range of emotions returning
To the night in the past

Perhaps, I was waiting for someone to turn up
Or, perhaps, I was merely sitting here, in order to drink
With a soul

水故宫

七月遇见暴雨
六十多年的癫狂
雷鸣粉碎一天闪电

从前门到钟鼓楼
从房山到石景山
洗刷了京城
然后声东击西

筒子河水一涨再涨
故宫，一块赭红的石头
在大水中漂浮

赤红的宫墙上
一道闪光
前朝的宫女太监
移动碎步
在四氧化三铁中浮现

紫禁城
被另一道闪电复活
风水轮流的24个帝王
趴在权力的水银深处
正忙着清洗真相的污渍
虚构岁月的伪风景

比如：幽禁南宫，落叶秋黄
比如：夺门之变，铅锁刀光
比如：梃击案、红丸案，案案腥红
比如：移宫风波，风波云涌

Summer Palace in Water

July hit by a storm
With a demented fury in 60-odd years
The thunder had shattered a sky of lightning flashes
From the Front Gate to the Clock Drum Tower
And from the House Hill to the Stone Scene Hill
Drenching the capital city
Before it moved west, pretending to attack east

The Bamboo Tube River, swelling again and again
Gave a tight hug to the multi-hued and flirtatious
Body of Summer
Palace, a red stone
Floating and drifting in the deluge
A ray of light flashing across
The scarlet palace wall
As the imperial concubines and eunuchs of previous dynasties
Emerged in the ferrous-ferric oxide
Moving in their chop-chop steps

Portraits of the dead, hanging from the edges of the skirts
Were revived in another flash of the lightning
The Forbidden City, in dragon robes
Was crouching in the depths of mercurial power
With its 24 emperors going by turns of wind and water
Busy cleansing the stains of truth
Fictionalizing the years in a pseudo landscape, such as

The imprisonment in Southern Palace, with fallen yellow leaves of autumn
Or the light of swords, locked in lead, for a change of Gates
Or the Baton Bashing in 1615 and the Red Pill in 1620, both bloody enough

床榻上一个左倾的懒腰
便人头落地
如七月的暴雨
一块块水的石头
在故宫
回光返照的寸砖片瓦上
倒流

水故宫，水故宫
叠着一个又一个
隐痛的漩涡
流水声声
粉饰山河

Or the surging waves involving the Relocation of Palace in the Ming Dynasty

A lazy stretching of one's legs in the bed
Would lead to heads rolling on the floor
Like the rainstorm in July
Stone after stone of water
Is flowing backwards
Over the inch of tiles or bricks
In the Summer Palace

Summer Palace in water, Summer Palace in water
Layered with one whirlpool after another
Its sound of flowing
Decorating the nation's mountains and waters

另一个世界的悲歌（组诗七首）
——写于1989年至1992年

一、摹拟春天

这一年春天，流言与厄运滂沱
一场喷出伤痕的雨季
湿润的火焰四处扩散
穿过每一个人的皮肉，走进三月
走进1990，这个破碎与怀旧的灵堂

流出绿光，摹拟的春夜
子弹在记忆里弯曲地飞，这个老手
在半路上停步，似是而非
瞄准星辰
打开一盏盏零零星星的灯

透过黑铁条的窗户
一小块，一小块的天空抱着桃树枝
在光线的每一根脊背上微微发抖
日子煎熬一天又一天
月色桃花散发清香的死讯

对于劫数，最敏感的事物泄露了
异样的表情，触动花园
那棵成年已久的黄桃树
皮开肉绽，为眼红的祖国滚出泪珠
明察秋毫的流言和苦难
坚定地，在一潭死水中彻夜闪烁

它丰满成熟的刀子
挖走我的心肝

Sad Songs from Another World
(A sequence of 7 poems)
– Written between 1989 and 1992

A. Mimicking the Spring

In the spring of that year, rumour and misfortune in bucket-loads
A rainy season, erupting from the scars
And going through everyone's skin, walks into March
Into 1990, the mourning hall of brokenness and nostalgia

The mimicked spring night, flowing with green light
The bullet flies, in a curved way, through memory, this old hand
Stops halfway, specious
Aimed at the stars
Switching on the sparse lamps, one after another

Tiny patches of the sky, through the black-iron-barred window
Are hugging the peach tree branches
Shivering on the back of every light
Day suffering by day
News of death on the clean scent of moon-colour and peach-flowers

Facing inexorable doom, things, most sensitive, reveal
An unusual expression, touching the yellow peach flower
Tree, mature for long, in the garden
Bruised and lacerated, with rolling tears for the red-eyed mother
Land, perspicacious rumour and misery
Firmly, twinkling in a pool of dead water throughout the night

Its plump and ripe knife
Has dug out my heart

没有声息，没有一丝声息
犹如远方雾中的牢房
给每一张黄脸烙下斑驳的印痕

一夜之间
一颗心朝憎恶炸裂
一粒粒垂落的肉松子
一屋书页上消失的文字
向所有的黑夜飞去

一片片花瓣，模样各异
逃离了枝叶
而逃离黑暗的人
像动乱被风波捞出来
投进井然秩序的高墙

这些攫取恶名，被定罪的肉体
这些活生生的——
变成石头的灵魂啊
使分离和判决在铁屋子里
拥抱雪亮的空气

被玷污的一群，脸青面黑
行尸走肉，随便几个词语落在纸上
就能让你们终生结冰
在劳改的世界
修饰一片青春的废墟

而你，承担悲剧和轻浮的角色
不过是某个夏日，别人牺牲的对象
如一阵火焰的呜咽
坠入了更远的远方

Without a sound, without the shred of a sound
Like the prison cell in the distant fog
Branding each and every yellow face with dappled traces

Overnight
A heart splinters towards disgust
One after another fallen pine nut of flesh
A house filled with pages of disappearing words
Flying towards all the dark nights

Petal after petal of flowers, in different appearances
Have escaped from their branches or leaves
And people, who have escaped from the darkness
Are scooped up by wind and wave like unrests
And are chucked behind the tall wall of good order

These bodies, convicted, that grabbed hold of an evil name
These living—
Souls that have turned into stones
Making departure and sentence embrace the snow-shining
Air in the iron house

The stigmatized group, of darkened faces
Walking corpses, random words that fell onto the paper
Would land you in perpetual ice
Furnishing the ruins of youth
In the world of reform through labour

And you, undertaking the role of tragedy and a flirt
Is a mere object for other people's sacrifice in a certain summer
Like the whimpering of a fire
Falling further into the distance

一些阴影飞来
你的面孔破碎
反动的罐头被撬开
随着走漏的空气变质
关节中煽动的风湿
在远东，宣传反革命的酸痛

如此的晕眩，正如一场流产的革命

顷刻间，广场水火不容
草皮尖叫，松针逃进温暖的弹壳
精通暴力的手腕
带着话筒，公章和火药的味道
用高压开口，万物喊痛

人类又一次用死亡练习急转弯
我浑身的毛孔垂挂愤怒
面向半个祖国下跪
——六月嚎啕大哭

明天，日子和岁月
将在哪一道闪电上喘息，拖着
这座城市被蒸干的躯体
一转身，比死亡更迅速更彻底

那里，紧锁的城堡！过分的光明摧毁了昼夜
那里，颠倒的头颅！渴望夜晚、厨房、女人
那里，骨肉的减法！黑夜是最大的奢侈
那里，模范的牢狱！人类最智慧的古迹

A number of shadows come flying
Your face shattered
The reactionary cans prized open
Deteriorating with the leaked air
The wind-wet rheumatism flapping in the joints
In the Far East, the sour-pain of propagandizing the anti-revolutionaries

Such dizziness, just like an aborted revolution

In an instant, the Square refused to contain water or fire
The turf was screaming and the pine needles ran into the warm bullet-shells
Wrists, versed in violence
Carrying loudspeakers, public seals and the smell of gunpowder
Opened their mouths with high pressure till things were crying pain

Once again, humanity practiced hairpin turns with death
Anger was hanging from all the pores of my body
As I went on my knees in the face of half a motherland
June burst into tears

Tomorrow, days, months and years
Which lightning will they pant on, dragging
The steam-dry body of this city
Faster and more thorough than death as it turns around?

There, the castle under lock and key! Excessive light having destroyed
night and day
There, the skull turned upside down! Hankering after night, kitchen and
woman
There, the reduction of bone and flesh! Night being the maximum luxury
There, a model prison! The most wise relic of humanity

二、永不到达的判决

比活着更久远的宣判遥遥无期
我的冤家，你的意外
在一个突然的上午，道德错乱的上午
被一颗管制的铁钉打进脑门
房子清冷，空气板着纠察的嘴脸
许多搬动诗歌这块敲门砖的兄弟
熟悉的面孔瞬间变成青色和惨白
敏捷的牙齿与舌尖
保持躲避的姿势
在风暴的尾巴拴上疏远和保险

传说的告密者
比嘴皮吧嗒的节奏
和细菌繁殖的速度更快
如同剧毒的鸿毛
穿过惊悸的人群
各种阴影飞来飞去

暗藏的血燕衔着汉语的把柄
与告密的唾液
带来一些穿透血丝的燕窝
这些红色昂贵的滋补品
一切都难以言说
我怎么能够逃避一个时代的标语

口号、语录、墙壁上大红的黑体
如同剥光皮肉的鱼
卡在日常生活的喉咙
而装满饥饿的胃，打着说谎的饱嗝
什么东西摸起来更真实，我的手

B. The Sentence that Never Arrives

The sentence, longer than being alive, is infinitely coming
My yuanjia-enemy, your unexpectedness
On a sudden morning, one with a deranged moral sense
A controlling nail was driven into the brains
A cold house, the air stiffening the security's mouths and faces
Familiar faces instantly turning into a dark and ghastly white
Agile teeth and tips of tongues
Kept a posture of avoidance
Tying the tail of the storm with remoteness and safety

The informants, as rumoured
Were quicker than the rhythms of lips zipping
And the proliferation of bacteria
Like poisoned feathers of wild swans
Going through startled crowds
All kinds of shadows flying about

Hidden blood-swallows, with the handle of the Chinese language in their beaks
And the phlegm of the informants
Brought edible birds' nests shot with shreds of blood
Everything too much for speech
How could I ever escape the posters of an age

Slogans, sayings, and black characters on the wall in bright red
Like fish stripped of their skin
Were stuck in the throat of ordinary lives
And, stomachs, filled with hunger, were belching with lies, pretending
to be filled
Something more real than felt, my hand
Stopped in the wind

停顿在风中
那唯一的时间的证据
像音乐的影子无踪无迹

许多突变的事件一夜粉碎
让我肝胆欲裂又心静如水
在受人摆布的疼痛里
我早就看见梦魇与死亡的根基

正如昨天爆发的骚乱，痛心疾首
一个躯体刚被折断
另一个躯体又被洞开
苍天流血，生命搁置在一张薄纸上
骨头咬着脱离的手臂
整座城市交错杂乱，呼吸残喘
人们在死亡身边奔逃传递
难以置信的杀伤力
血腥开花的国都
死神也懒得抬一抬眼皮

这个特殊、悲凉的时候
我可以牺牲一切，想一想你
我的冤家，你遭浪费的生命
你轻狂、毫无原则的一生
此刻坐在另一群人，另一个凶险的世界
你的心是否比我更痛

街灯卖弄的光亮耻笑遗忘
这座劫后余生的城市，依然舒适安逸
惶惑的锅底，油爆在街心翻腾
人们收拾起过期的绝食和精神呕吐
在变质的血腥中
踩着恶习，继续前行

The only evidence of time
Traceless, like the shadow of the wind

Many sudden incidents were shattered overnight
Ripping my liver apart and rendering my heart as quiet as water
In the pain of being ruled
I had long seen the nightmares and the foundation of death

Like the turmoil that broke out yesterday, one was devastated
That one body had just got broken
And another, opened with a gaping hole
The ancient sky was bleeding, lives placed on a thin piece of paper
Bones were biting the detached hands and arms
A whole city in a mess, where breathing was left lingering
People were running around death conveying
Incredible power of hurting
In the capital of the nation, blooming in blood
Not even the King of Death would bother raising its eyelids

In this special, sad moment
I could sacrifice everything in giving a thought to you
My yuanjia-enemy, your wasted life
A life wild and unprincipled
Right now, another group of people sitting, in another dangerous world
Is your heart more sore than mine?

The lights the street lamps were selling scorned forgetfulness
This city, that has had a close brush with death, remains comfortable and
at ease
At the bottom of the bewildered woks, sizzling rose in the heart of the streets
People put away obsolete hunger-strikes and spiritual vomiting
In the stale bloodbath
Kept forging ahead, treading their evil habits

历史，这张油彩善变的花脸
周而复始，朝朝夕夕
火焰的枝叶依然美得过火
燃烧的王后在时间的油汤下
更加猩红，翻滚

咽喉留在一支长笛的
伤口中，慢曲调地吹
正如永不到达的判决
就要毁掉你脆弱、虚幻的前半生

History, the flowery face with changeable makeup
Repeats itself, day and night
The fiery branches are still excessively beautiful
The burning princess, in the oily soup of time
Is more scarlet, rolling around

The throat, staying in the wound
Of a long flute, blowing a slow tune
About to destroy your fragile, illusory half-life
Like the sentence that never arrives

三、火车站，狂乱的子夜

火车北站，子夜的牙缝
一具空洞的肉体挂上时间的弯钩
夜晚忙忙碌碌，马不停蹄
尖叫拖着包裹纠缠不清
歪倒一片的瞌睡，蓬头垢面
像随意飞出的黏痰
唾弃在闷热的水泥地
恶臭在嘴里燃烧，膨胀
两排黄金板牙咬紧拥挤
车门打开
人们过度慌张，用贫贱的蛮力
抢占一个可怜的位置

远走高飞的昨天
一个热爱离别的情人，看透一切
一滴美德的泪珠坠入了深渊
本质沉默着，隐忍不语
当民族的内衣被子弹加速的威风突然掀开
哦，时代戒严的牺牲品
吃苦耐劳的芸芸众生
抽空的灵魂如一片阴影扫过我的天空

哦，囚犯！罪与罚的风景
打着折扣的生日
在一具铁棺内磨皮擦痒
瞧，灯火通明中你们的手脚
苍白如一张过期的废纸
墙外的一切，遥不可及
另一个空间，另一个维度
在内部，在地底

C. The Railway Station, a Wild Midnight

At the Northern Railway Station, the seams of midnight's teeth
A hollow body hanging from the curved hook of time
Busy night, like an unstoppable horse
Screaming, dragging bags, got entangled
A sleep of fallen askanceness, dirty faces with disheveled hair
Like the sticky phlegm that shot at random
Only to be left on the stiflingly hot cement
Stink burning, swelling, in the mouth
Two rows of gold teeth biting hard, squeezing
As the doors opened
People got so panicky, scrambling for a pitiable seat
With their abject brutal force

Yesterday, high flown and far flung
A lover in love with departure, who had seen through everything
A drop of moral tear, fallen into the abyss
What was essential kept silent, wordless
When the underclothes of a nation were lifted, on a sudden, by the
quickening bullets
Well, victims of an age of enforced martial law
All mortal beings able to eat bitterness and endure hardships
Their depleted souls, like a shadow, swept my sky

Ah, the prisoner! Landscape of crime and punishment
A discounted birthday
Scratching your itchiness in an iron coffin
Look: your hands and feet, in the bright lights
As white as a piece of dated paper
Everything outside the wall unreachable
Another space, another dimension

鬼魅的镣铐放风自由
钻进皮肉和心肺，洋洋自得
像阴沟里的皇帝

那钩子上的皇后
悬挂着老祖宗
眼珠肿胀，忧伤昏黄
抓住两片云烟
不分昼夜抖动
没有惊喜也没有失望
像命早已呈现在昨天
整个世界躲躲闪闪

火车北站哀诉的钟声敲破喉咙
攒动的人头和粪便堆满
心在几个小钱中搅动，自怜
过早拥挤的脸，拥挤
在咳嗽的空气中
在沸腾的地皮上
人们像一堆苦难的标本，活的遗骸
蚊子和苍蝇盘旋在裸露的关节
玩耍，交尾

卷入人类悲伤的列车
在世纪末的铁轨上失去了知觉
昼夜呻吟的枕木
疲劳的车笛，呜的一声
从天堂滑到了地狱
从愤怒冲向仇人的心窝
我的命摔在半空，血在快速挥发
不安的意象，粉碎的星星
塞满了我的行李
赶快，霜耗泛滥的城市

In the inside, at the bottom of the earth
Fetters of ghosts let out for exercise, for free
Creeping into the skin and the heart, pleased with themselves
Like the emperor in the ditch

The empress, on the hook
A hanging Old Ancestor
With swollen eyeballs, sad and yellow
Clutching two pieces of Yunnan tobacco
Shaking them day and night
With no delight, no disappointment
Like fate that had presented itself the day before
The whole world dodging

The whining bell in the Northern Railway Station broke the throat
Surging heads heaped with dung
Hearts stirring amidst coins, self-pitying
Faces, getting crowded too early, crowding
In the coughing air
On the boiling skin of the earth
People were like samples of misery, remains of the living
Mosquitoes and flies were hovering around the naked joints
Playing, tail-coupling

The train, sucked into the saddened humanity
Lost its consciousness on the tracks of the fin-de-siecle
The sleepers moaning day and night
The fatigued whistle, giving a hoot
Slid from heaven to hell
Rushing from fury to the heart of the enemies
My fate, dashed mid-air, blood quickly evaporating
Uneasy images, smashed stars
Stuffed my luggage

紧跟哄闹的人头一路收集失败
就要到站了，铁轨摩肩击毂
精通暴力的人类
就要到站了，漆黑空荡的四周
突然比屠杀还要热烈
掀起混乱，冷酷，拥挤的旋风
向停靠三分钟的火车汹涌
猛冲车门的人群，一阵阴风
掩盖了狂乱的心

Quick! In a city flooded with bad news
Follow the noisy heads all the way to collect failure
Arriving soon, the tracks scraping shoulders
Human beings, versed in violence
Would be arriving soon, in the surrounding darkness
It suddenly became more heated than butchery
A vortex of confusion, cruelty and crowd
Surging towards the train, stopped only for 3 minutes
The crowd pounding the door, a blowing of chilling wind
Covered the wild hearts

四、驶向深渊的都市

这是一连串噩梦
一节一节扣着无边的呻吟
挤上硬座的躯体，药黄的面容
餐盒、塑料纸袋，隔夜的烧酒
记忆，幻想，麻痹，垂死
廉价的大嘴广播恶浊的英雄主义
铁轨，这狂欢与苦难轮回的怪圈
　　呼哧呼哧

用它厌恶的蹄子碾动，碾动
一节扣一节，锈蚀的铁皮
被油漆涂得发绿，夜
像一个凄楚、贪婪的老妇
弥天的围裙越来越肮脏，黑暗
在众目睽睽下，一股肥如专制的暴风
裹走了白天仅有的绣花胸衣
人们在内心的地狱，冷沙一样碎裂
灯丝向细菌弯曲，火焰惩罚微笑
把瞌睡到极点的旅程烧得疼痛
　　呼哧呼哧

一节扣一节，滚动向前的坟冢
轮子上晃动的牢狱
从深渊的都市，伸展粗暴
伸展极速生死
卑劣与暴力嫁接出政治的双刃
破绽百出的捆绑和拘留
如造句
随意插入一段个人的日常生活
使岁月感染，隐痛

D. The Metropolis Driven into the Abyss

This is a series of nightmares
Buttoning up endless moanings, one by one
Bodies squeezing themselves onto the hard seats, medicine-yellow faces
Lunchboxes, plastic paper bags, burning liquor left from last night
Cheap mouths broadcasting the filthy heroism
Railway tracks, the weird cycle of mad excitement and misery
      Puffing and panting, panting and puffing

Grinding and grinding, with their disgusted hooves
The rusty skins of iron, section by section
Were painted green, the night
Like a wretched, greedy old woman
Her apron extended to cover up the sky, became dirtier, in the darkness
Stared at by the public, a storm as fat as the dictatorship
Took away the only laced bra, owned by the day
In the hell of their own hearts, people broke into pieces, like cold sands
Filaments of a lamp were bending themselves towards bacteria, the fire
                                              punishing
The smiles, burning the extremely sleepy journey, till it became painful
      Puffing and panting, panting and puffing

One section following another, the tomb that was rolling forward
A jail on wheels
Roughness extended itself from the abysmal metropolis
Extending extreme life and death
The double edges of politics grafted on despicable violence
The tying up and detention, full of loopholes
Like sentences made
Inserted, randomly, into the ordinary life of an individual
Infecting the years, the hidden pain

飞快分泌出
厌恶的疥疮颗粒
如同墓穴中风干的眼珠
活着比死更没有生气
　　　呼哧呼哧

没有终结，是开始，仅仅
不要惊慌，撒旦先生
罪恶谣言的日子，水银中的一滴
明目张胆飞来星星点点
一群夏天淫乱的虫子
传递着牢房压弯的耳语
灰暗的命运倚靠猥琐，打着瞌睡
另一个世界揉着眼睛，生活越来越模糊
更多碎裂的意象与焊接的声音
一个比一个更残暴更盲目
一夜之间统统掉进世纪末
这个假眠的大时代
万物犯困，伸着懒腰
唯有一双破旧沾满尘土的小布鞋
从酣睡的脚上重重地落到了地面
　　　呼哧呼哧

车厢沉闷的缝隙，锁链着深夜
无尽奔忙在路上，真理拆迁了爱
归途更加遥远
人们彼此芥蒂、怨恨
种种罪行隐匿
被内心的国家判处终生苦役
悲凉和孤寂驻定我的心中
无奈鼓起青筋
手背和额头突出在肉体的遗址上
失眠的夜灯使书页上的文字燃烧

Secreting, flyingly quick
The disgusting grains of scabies
Like wind-dried eyeballs in the graves
Living is more unliving than death
    Puffing and panting, panting and puffing

No ending, only, a beginning,
Stop panicking, Mr Satan
Days of criminal rumours, a drop of quick silver
Dots and sparks that came flying with flagrance
A crowd of obscene summary insects
Passed around the bent whispers of the prison cell
The fate, grey and dark, was dozing away, relying on wretchedness
Another world was rubbing its eyes as life became more obscure
More broken images and welded sounds
One more ruthless and blind than the other
Falling towards the end of the century overnight
In this great age of pretended sleep
Things grew weary, stretching themselves
Only a small pair of cloth shoes, worn and covered in dust
Fell off the soundly asleep feet, heavily onto the floor
    Puffing and panting, panting and puffing

The depressing seams of the compartments, chained to the deep night
Busy rushing endlessly on the road, as truth had relocated love
And the journey back became farther away
Ill feelings and resentment between people
Crimes of all sorts hidden away
One was sentenced to bitter life imprisonment by the nation within
Desolation and solitude took roots in my heart
Veins stood out with helplessness
The back of the hand and the forehead prominent on the ruins of flesh
The night, insomniac, set the words alight on the page

一些汉字的灰烬，如一小片
一小片黑雪，将我引向另一个世界
门庭半开，像我多年来临时栖居的小屋
简单、随和又动荡不安
　　　呼哧呼哧

这是我一生最黑暗的日子
此时，我在外地的哪一节车厢
发着高烧，剧烈咳嗽
污言秽语从四周霉烂的气味爬出来
像死囚发黏的骨灰爬过我的耳根
暗处游走的扒手，绞尽脑汁
怀揣窃国的地图，满城风雨
从梦中偷走了我的阳光和健康
"什么东西那么晕眩，刺眼，强盗！"
"一颗子弹穿心而过！"
　　　呼哧呼哧

Ashes of a few Chinese characters, like a small patch
A small patch of black snow, led me to another world
The door ajar, like the hut I had taken temporary residence in for many years
Was simple, casual and restless
      Puffing and panting, panting and puffing

This is the darkest day of my life
At this very moment, I am in a compartment in the provinces
In high fever, coughing violently
Dirty language crept out from the surrounding moldy smell
Past the root of my ears, like the sticky ashes of the prisoner sentenced
                                              to death
Pickpockets, moving about furtively, racking their brains
Harbouring a map to steal the nation, in a city filled with wind and rain
Have stolen my sunshine and health
'What is it that is so dizzy, so eye-dazzling, Robber!'
'A bullet that passes through the heart!'
      Puffing and panting, panting and puffing

五、四月在下坠

那里，有人坐在四季的笼中
孤单而清淡的样子
一抬头，满树的桃花潸然泪下
一个倾斜的社会背剪双手
绑到了南方，下石板坡

犹如一只黑兽嚼碎的阴影
一副不痛不痒的表情
一块处子大腿上安静的小污点
突然飘荡天外，一炉火焰
燃烧的花瓣从身后照亮了你粗糙的世界
这个犯罪的港湾，停靠无声无息
死亡像少女流产一样平常、简单

而四月，是一个春天的碎嘴婆
比三月更露骨更猖狂更花枝招展
风中一个个七零八落的吻
无力地奔向你笼中的窗户
一颗纸做的心贴满了嘴唇
从坡上的牢房飞了下来
落在我吃尽苦头的膝盖

仿佛更多的器官在哭泣
像荆棘四处漫游
淫荡的四月流淌在两腿之间
把黄昏插进没有戒备的空瓶
春天的毒素沿着发根渗进我头脑的深处

没有一丝疼痛
只听见某种声音在坠下，在开始

E. April is Sinking

There, someone is sitting in the cage of four seasons
Looking single and delicate
As soon as she looks up, the peach flowers filling the tree shed their tears
A slanting society, its arms behind its back
Is taken, bound, to the south, down the flagstone slope

Like a shadow, chewed into shreds, by a black animal
An expression of neither painful nor itchy
A quiet dirty dot on the thigh of a virgin
On a sudden, drifts beyond the sky, a stove of fires
Its burning petals lights up your rough world
This criminal harbour, berthing without a sound
Death ordinary, and simple, like the abortion of a girl

And April, a gossipy woman of spring
Is more bone-naked, more aggressive, more stunning than March
Kisses, at sixes and sevens, in the wind
Rushing, without strength, towards your window in the cage
A heart, made of paper, is pasted with lips
Comes flying down from the prison on the slope
To my knees that have eaten so much bitterness

More organs, it seems, are crying
Wandering around, like the thorns
The obscene April is oozing between the legs
Thrusting the dusk into the unguarded bottle of emptiness
Poison of the spring is seeping in the depth of my brains along the roots

Not a shred of pain
All one can ever hear is the fall of a certain sound, that is beginning to

在斜穿而过，一只神经的老虎
呵，神经，纸，四月暗藏的老虎
破门而入
星星跌进眼底，额头滚烫
我的生活在夜晚用了两年的时间失眠

Pass through, diagonally, a nervous tiger

Ah, nervous, paper, a tiger hidden in April

Crashes the door

As the stars fall to the bottom of the eyes, the forehead heating up

My life has spent two years being insomniac at night

六、飞行的间谍

一枚细小的月亮，在花间
草地上昼夜飞行
阴天踢破了门槛
受伤的气息溜进我的肺腑
一股被捆住的呼吸，突然
从五月的背后潜入我的鼻孔

现在，光天化日之下
只有这间九平方米的小屋
叩着羞愧的手指
看见一整天，看见每一秒
都在受迫害中冲动

装满信封和诗稿的抽屉四脚朝天
碎花的被子裹着枕巾洒落一地
我的手不能像羽毛飞的更高
越过一屋绝望的家具
越过这片被迫害被追捕的风景

而你早已消失
连一个词，一个嘴唇的翕动
也来不急
当我借助一条又旧又脏的裙子
穿越一屋警察的时刻
我仅仅是一个无辜的女子
而那些被我藏进衣裙的书信
早就料到了以后的悲剧

五月，一个平常的月份
间谍在空气中横行

F. The Flying Spy

A tiny moon is flying, amongst the flowers
And over the lawn, day and night
The overcast weather kicks in the threshold
A smell, hurt, creeps in my heart
A breath, tied up, suddenly
Penetrates my nostrils from behind May

Now, in broad daylight
This tiny room, of only nine square meters
Knocking its ashamed fingers
Sees the whole day, the whole second
Getting impulsive when persecuted

The drawers, filled with envelopes and poetry manuscripts, have feet up
in the sky
The quilt, of broken flowers, with a pillow-towel in it, is scattered on the
floor
My hands cannot fly higher than the feathers
Across a house of furniture in despair
Across this landscape of persecution and pursuit

And you have long disappeared
Without even time for words, for the moving
Of a lip
When I, in a skirt old and dirty
Went through a room full of policemen
I was only an innocent woman
And those letters, hidden in my skirt
Had expected what tragedy would ensue

美丽的假牙，带着感冒的亲吻
我触碰到她怀中的银针
当她含着糖果
招摇过市
一把充满酸味的星星也被揪着
爆发间谍的高烧
像一只刺猬尖端的微笑
这些昼夜奔涌的星星们啊
从来都没有终结
啊，这个跳跃的年代
这个喜欢错误的时代
我们多么丑陋，多么天真

In May, an ordinary month
Spies were on a rampage in the air
Beautiful false teeth, kissing with a cold
I touched the silver needles in her arms
When she swaggered through the street
A candy in her mouth
A handful of stars, filled with sour tastes, were also gripped
Breaking in a spy's fever
Smiling the sharp smile of a hedgehog
Ah, these stars that were surging day and night
Never with an end
Ah, this age of leaping
This age addicted to mistakes
How ugly, how innocent we are!

七、世纪末，一个唯心的初夏

山城，爬坡上坎的房舍
街道、拐角，在世纪末患了偏头痛
一张发锈早衰的脸
沾满灰垢，召唤死亡
小洞天火锅夜夜火爆
毛肚、黄喉、鸭肠
冒着青烟左倾，风卷残云
这个唯心的初夏，主义出逃海外
我一个人长途搬运悲苦，通向狱堡
企图在发烧的城市偿还死神的债务
妄想，危情加速

背着隆起的祭祀和六月莽撞的山河
我提前两个小时，爬过饥饿
爬上下石板坡
记忆从水泥地面揭起，旧痛隐隐发作
石缝挤出几棵荒草，头顶藏匿
费九牛二虎之力，我挤进
一扇铁门
偏西的小屋，看守，警察叔叔
像室内古怪的音乐
用枯燥，不耐烦的降 f 小调
呼叫着如卷心菜，葱头，青菜疙瘩
一样混乱冷漠
嘀嘀咕咕的犯人家属

瞧，我一身飘雪的衣裙
素白的蕾丝，用尽了力气纯洁
使几颗穿制服的头颅，坐在椅子上有些内疚
一束向外张望的茉莉花握紧疼痛

G. Early Summer of Idealism, the End of the Century

In the mountain city, the house that one has to reach by climbing a slope
And turning corners, is suffering from migraine at the end of the century
A face, rusty, decaying for long
And stained with dust, is calling for death
The fire woks at Little Hole Sky are cracking every night
Hairy belly, Yellow Throat, Duck's Intestines
Smoking with left tendencies, while wind is rolling up the residual clouds
In this early summer of idealism, isms are running overseas
Alone, I move sadness long distance, towards the castle of prisons
Attempting to pay off the debt to death in a feverish city
Willful thinking, danger speeding
Shouldering the bulging sacrifices and rash mountains and rivers of June
I, two hours ahead of time, creep across hunger
Across the lower flagstone slope

As memory is lifted from the cement surface and old pain is ready to
break out
A cluster of wild grasses squeeze themselves out of the stone seams, hidden
overhead
I, with the strength of nine oxen and two tigers, push myself
Through an iron door
A hut in the west wing, guarded by Uncle Policemen
Like the weird music in the room
Yelling, in boring
F flat minor, as confusing and cold
As Chinese cabbage, bulb onion and knotted green vegetables
Chatting family members of the prisoner

Look at my garments with drifting snow
Pure white lace, trying my best to be pure

握紧划破掌心的愤怒
在看守所的接待室释放出寂静的光
这不是儿戏，芬芳的花朵
值得浪费，为了
几盒香烟和抄写几个昼夜的
《杜英诺的悲歌》能够送到
那双被贫血凝固的手里
看守的眼珠在书籍上扫荡，乱象丛生
我在心中为你朗读
这个一错再错，凶兆流淌的年代
深夜，我一个人
把苦难压缩，放进抽屉
诗歌是我的口粮，等候是我青黄不接的稻谷

"嘿嘿！茉莉花？这是什么地方？"
"这是蹲狱"他们权力的话语
让满屋尘埃冒出虚汗，我屏住气
这里，一扇铁门主宰斜坡上的命运
戒备森严的狱堡挤满了
标着数码的身躯
青春被塞进门角
意志卷入任意一捆拖布
在被剥夺，被管制的地面
扫来扫去
这些打着数码的肉体
只有一个名字：囚徒

我再一次刨出语言的糖衣
裹着良心的血滴，像一枚闲棋冷子
对弈他们，山核桃一般坚硬的心
而这一次
一个被嘲笑的天使
飞翔的嗅觉

Causing the heads in uniform to feel guilty in their chairs
A bunch of jasmine flowers, looking outside, is tightly gripping hold of pain
Of the anger that cuts open the palm
A quiet light is released from the reception room in the detention centre
It's no children's play; fragrance of the flowers
Is worth the waste, all for the purpose
Of a few cigarette packs and the copy of Duino Elegies, days and nights
So that they could reach
The hands congealing with anemia
The eyeballs of the guard are mopping up the books, an exuberant growth of
Confused images. I am reading for you, from my heart
This age that wrongs after wrong, flowing with ill omens
Deep at night, I, alone
Compress the misery and put it in the drawer
Poetry is my rationed food and, awaiting me, is the grains of rice not yet ripe

'Hay, Jasmine, what is this place?'
'This is sitting in a jail,' the power of their discourse
Let the room sweat weak sweat, I hold my breath
Here, an iron door has dominated the fate on the slope
The maximum security prison castle is filled
With numbered bodies
Youth stuffed into a corner
Will randomly rolled into a mop
Sweeping to and fro
On the floor of deprivation and control
These numbered bodies
Have only one name: Prisoner

Once again, I dig out the sugared-clothes of language
Wrapped with the blood-drops of conscience, like a cold chess piece
Playing against them, my heart, as hard as a mountain walnut
And this time

夹满了悲伤与感动的翅膀
越过两层楼高的空气
闻到了你秃头的气息

如果你渺小弯曲的灵魂
注定要撞入秋天的虎口
在夏日的深处
谁的命运将越来越残酷
谁的忧伤？谁的眼泪
将落得更轻，更远，更辽阔

The flying smell
Of a scorned angel
Is sandwiched between sadness and moved wings
Smelling the smell of your bald head
From the air that is two-storey high

If your insignificant and bent soul
Is destined to bump into the tiger's mouth in the autumn
In the depth of the summer then
Whose fate will become crueler
And whose sadness? Whose tears
Will drop lighter, farther, and vaster?

内心的粮食、水果、花蜜

这些日子我闭门不出
北风在窗外卷起是非与尘土
寒冷的冬天
我灌满一袋温水暖脚
读仓央嘉措的情诗与你的书信暖心

你早年缺衣少穿的身世
与那个夜晚华丽的细节背道而驰
北风呼啸的冬天
你让我围着一盆心火，通体带电
我毫无准备地爱上了你

只能把内心的粮食、水果与花蜜
统统搬运出来，义无反顾地
走向了那条拥有你的私密小道

（2011年元月27日晨）

Food, Fruit and Nectar, in My Heart of Hearts

Over the last few days, I stayed behind a closed door
As the northerly was stirring up trouble and dust
A cold winter
In which I warmed my feet with a bag of warm water
And I warmed my heart, with love poems of Cangyang Gyatso and your letters

Your early life, with little clothing
Ran counter to the florid details of that night
In a winter of roaring northerly
When you got me to surround a basin of heart fire, my whole person electrified
And when I, without any preparation, fell in love with you

All I could do is bring out all the food, fruit and nectar
From my heart of hearts, and, without any hesitation
Make for the private path that owns you

(morning, 27/01/2011)

心空

刮风下雨是自然的变化
爱与不爱是心情的变化
你一走，心就空了
留下一粒患得患失的种子

你可以用酒泼掉自己的余生
也可以用借口注解不幸
我从来的路上被迫后退，一步踏空
却步入了藏满虫鸣与树林的天涯

想一想，人情渐薄
真爱一场
两颗心的巧合
足够一个人跋涉一生

于是我放下心来
自食其果，回头
在诗篇中用想象把你爱到极致
是我自己的事

（2011年2月12日清晨）

Heart Hollow

It's a natural change for wind to blow and for rain to rain
And it's a heart's change to love and not to love
When you left, my heart was emptied
With a seed kept, afraid of gains and losses

You can pour out the rest of your life with wine
And also annotate misfortunes with excuses
But I'm forced to retreat from my erstwhile path, stepping into the
emptiness
And further into the edge of the sky where chirpings of insects and trees
are hidden

Just think: while feelings are thin
And true love comes
Two hearts that have met by chance
Are enough for one person to trudge a whole life

So, I put my heart down
To eat my own fruit, self-sown, and turn my head back
To imagine your love, in a poem, to the extreme
And it's none of your business

(Early morning, 12/2/2011)

空气 水滴 沙子

她被自己汹涌的爱窒息
仅凭一次措手不及的命运
一念之差便用一个形容词
撑起落花流水

走到哪里
就把哗哗流淌的心事
带到哪里

她要的亲吻与拥抱
本来就是镜中花
倾向于在水中回避的月色

她只能劝说自己
把无限的爱用窗外
那场推迟的大雪牵挂起来

然后，把灵魂的镜子
再次擦拭，瞧，寂静中
她不再奢求什么
比雪片还通透，干净

从情人那里退隐
从一朵忧伤到一个圣婢
她只爱着
像空气、水滴、沙子

（2011年2月14日深夜）

Air, Water-drops, Sands

Asphyxiated by her own tempestuous love
And via a fate that took her by storm, she
On the strength of a wrongful thought, held up the fallen flowers
In the flowing waters, with an adjective

Wherever she went
She would carry her humming
Heart matters

The kisses and hugs she wanted
Were, after all, flowers in the mirror
Colours of the moon that tended to be evaded in the water

All she could do is persuade herself
To hang the limitless love with the delayed
Snow outside the window

Then, wiping the soul's mirror
Again. Look, in the stillness
She, more transparent than the snowflakes, and cleaner
No longer desires anything

Retiring from her lover
From a sorrow to a sacred maid
All she loves appears
Like air, water-drops, sands

(Late night, 14/2/2011)

半壁山河

命中带足六点水的潇潇
在汉语词典的某一页
水深而清，风平浪静
而唐朝积满泪水的落木
飘在我名字的河床上全都绿了
我丰腴起来的肢体
面对时间的皇帝，有些羞愧
被光阴流淌成一颗珍珠中的江湖

在江湖的反光中
你背靠亲密的山峰
把半颗心投下
让我的水域一涨再涨
带水的世界都向你倾斜
水涨船高

你又把江山在我的腰部
一分为二
你拥有了我
就得到了半壁山河
不信，伸出左手
芳草连天，江水滚滚而来

你的掌心紧握着我
剑走偏锋，心事过重
幸与不幸仅一线之差
最爱的人易在自己内心遇难
见与不见，都暗流涌动
你灵魂的半壁山河依然是我

（2011年3月4日夜）

Half the Mountain and the River

A life full of six drops of water as in 潇潇
On a certain page in a Chinese dictionary
The water is deep and clean, the wind flat, the waves quiet
And the fallen woods, soaked with tears, in the Tang dynasty
Have all greened, drifting on the riverbed of my name
My limbs, now plump
Are somewhat shy, in the face of Emperor Time
Turned into the river and lake in a pearl by the yin light

In the reflection of the rivers and lakes
You, with your back against the intimate mountain peak
Throw down half a heart
Raising my waters higher and higher
When the water-carrying world is all tilted towards you
Where a boat is higher on the rising waters

And you cut the mountain and the river in half
At my waist
Once you own me
You own half the mountain and the river
If you don't believe, hold out your left hand
The river waters will come rolling, with fragrant grasses connected to the skies

The heart of your palm holds me in a tight grip
A sword with a skidding blade, heart matters overweight
And a thread-wide difference between fortune and misfortune
It's easy for the one, loved best, to perish in one's own heart of hearts
Meeting or not meeting, dark currents surge
And half the mountain and the river of your soul remains me

(Night, 4/3/2011)

她的河流

夜深人静，另一个世界
就躲在耳朵里
她像一枚失眠症的贝壳
在一浪一浪句子的波涛上
荡来荡去

她冒失地把味道最好的词语
放进嘴里
轻轻一咬
惊涛从唇齿间向一首诗
深不可测地甩出

那些香气中的记忆与宿命
都向南游移
那些皮肤上唱歌的气息
转向遥远
幸福又辛酸

她只好把一滴一滴
微咸，软软的水状物
用一个一个汉字吸干
靠在这个骨瘦的句子上
稳住脚跟，剪裁心情

想一想，那肉体深处
降生的云朵与光束
她的河流又开始流淌了……

（2011年3月8日晨）

Her River

Night deep. People quiet. Another world
Hides itself in the ears
Like a shell suffering from insomnia, she
Is drifting, to and fro
On the wave of lines, one after another

Brashly, she puts the best tasty words
In her mouth
And, with a gentle bite
Astounding waves gush from between her teeth
Fathomlessly towards a poem

Memory and fate
Wander southward
While breathings, sung on the skin
Turn to the faraway
Happy and bitter

She then has to suck dry
Drop after drop of watery stuff
Soft and slightly salty, with Chinese characters
Leaning against this bone-thin line
And standing on my own two heels, tailoring my heart-feelings

Just think: in the depths of the body
Clouds and clusters of light that were born
Her river, again, begins flowing...

(Morning, 8/3/2011)

树叶在等我

分手吧，亲爱的
毒瘤、坏脾气看守你
一个星期，六天缺席
我两手攥紧
这句话收藏了很久
一经出口
心爬满了虫子
美沦陷
如雀斑一样模糊的生活
没关系
树叶在风中等我

（2012年6月29日）

Leaves are Waiting for Me

Let's split up, my dear
A poisonous tumour and bad temper guard you
For a whole week, you have been absent for six days
My hands holding themselves tightly
As soon as the words, put aside for a long time
Are uttered
My heart is creeping with the insects
Beauty fell
A life as obscure as freckles
But it doesn't matter
Leaves are waiting for me in the wind

(29/6/2012)

秋天深处的妹妹

在秋天深处的妹妹
心凉了
被语言的黄金灼伤
流放到金枝玉叶上

在气候心脏的妹妹
有一种情怀比季节更深长
被一柄亮剑放逐
在摇晃的火焰上远走他乡

（2007年10月24夜）

Sister in the Depths of the Autumn

Sister in the depths of the autumn
Her heart has gone cold
Burnt by the gold of language
And sent into exile on the golden branches and jade leaves

Sister in the heart of climate
Has feelings deeper and longer than the seasons
Banished by a shining sword
She goes far away, on a shaking flame

(Night, 24/10/2007)

天赐的爱

南迦巴瓦山峰的雪
在十月
被阳光追赶的那个下午
纷纷落进我记忆的山谷

顺着你的手势
我的心被悄悄打开
群山朝我飞翔
秋风阵阵
吹得更轻、更快、更随心所欲

时间光着脚丫，掀开云彩
毫无保留地把全世界的金子
倾洒在南迦巴瓦雪山的最高处

（2007年3月8日晨7点）

Love, Blessed by the Sky

Snow on the Namjagbarwa
In October
And the afternoon, chased after by the sunlight
Are falling into the valley of my memory

With your gesture
My heart is, quietly, opened
As the crowd of mountains flies towards me
With rolls of autumnal wind
That blows lighter, faster and following its own bent more

Time, barefoot, is lifting the clouds
And scattering gold of all the world, without reserve
On the highest point of the Namjagbarwa

(7am, 8/3/2007)

午夜踮着脚尖

我的泪
在天上打转
就要落下一场倾盆大雨
午夜踮着脚尖
生怕打湿了裤脚

我形单影只
四周高楼的灯火
零零星星陪伴我到最后
在耗尽前，让幸福在阵痛中
再一次苏醒

当死亡踩着枯叶
来到枕边
一切的苦难和痛楚
都将成为感恩的部分

（2007年10月5日）

Midnight on Tiptoes

My tears
Are turning in the sky
As a pouring rain is about to fall
Midnight on tiptoes
Afraid of its trouser legs getting wet

I am a solitary figure, with a single shadow
Lights in the high rises around me
Keep me sporadic company till the last
Letting happiness wake up again
In the throes, before they consume themselves

When death comes to the side of my pillow
Treading the withered leaves
All the pain and sorrow
Will become part of thanksgiving

(5/10/2007)

时光流下的痛

你一次次抱歉说骚扰我
可为什么还要?
你让我记忆混乱、生气、歇斯底里
每一次放下电话
我更语无伦次,求求你
放下心上那团持久的灰烬
被霜打之后
我想停止所有的磨损
裹紧命运的毛边
变成另一片微不足道的叶子

(2009年9月13日凌晨2点)

Pain that Flows out of Time

You keep apologizing about harassing me
But why do you still want it?
You confuse my memory, making me angry and hysterical
Each time I put down the phone
I became more incoherent. I beg you
To put down the mess of lasting dust in the heart
Chipped by frost
I want to stop all the teardowns
And wrap the hairy edges of fate
To turn into an insignificant leaf

(2am, 13/9/2009)

暗香与死

转过身，还来不及抬腿
眼泪就先迈出了半步
有一种冷，一下子扫荡了全身
像今秋这场突然的大雪
把潮湿与羞耻推进心坎

那一串串泪水从花园
一直落到十楼
落到那些在厨房等待第二天
下锅的蚕豆、排骨
与鲁花花生油上

都是时间的错
这些年，谁的眼泪
悄悄养活了文字
谁的心血被捏在手中变成漩涡
全球化的非典、H5N1，咳嗽，咳嗽
只有暗香与死，一刹那
露出碎片的喜悦

（2009年11月6日晨）

Hidden Fragrance and Death

Turning around, and before I raised my leg
My tears had stepped out half a step
A coldness swept over my whole person
Like the big snow of this autumn
Pushing wetness and shame right into my heart

Strings of tears fell from the garden
Right down to the tenth floor
Onto the hyacinth beans, pork ribs and Luhua peanut oil
Waiting in the kitchen to go into the wok the next day

Blame the time
For, over the years, whose tears
Quietly kept alive the words
And whose heart-blood, held in the hand, turned into vortexes
Globalised SARS, H5N1, coughing and coughing
Except the hidden fragrance and death that, in an instant
Reveal the delight of fragrances

(Morning, 6/11/2009)

一朵玫瑰与中秋月
——致友人们

天快黑的时候
住在山坡上的友人
带来了康乃馨、百合花
和一朵红玫瑰

一大束芬芳开在众人脸上
满屋活色生香
那孤芳的一朵
正经过姐姐升起火苗的心

姐姐陶醉的嘴唇
把隐痛留在花瓣上
她说：那是意义不确定的一朵
却很喜悦和珍贵

加一的快递波浪翻滚
拍打着另一个让花儿抖得厉害的下午
让中秋的月色有些迟钝
有些手足无措

我每天打扫灵魂
为那朵寄养的玫瑰剪枝，置换清水
起身，换一套茉莉香的衣裙
等候友人们分享一盒"全聚德"的月光

那一朵玫瑰与中秋月
挂在我们几个心上
有些躲躲闪闪
是否梦见了宇宙外的山水与柴火

A Rose and the Mid-autumn Moon

– for my friends

Before it got dark
Friends living in the hills
Brought in carnation, lilies
And a red rose

A large bunch of fragrance was open on all the faces
In a house filled with live colours and scents
The single solitary fragrance
Was passing through Sister's heart where a flame was rising

Sister's lips, intoxicated
Kept her pain on a petal
And she said: That's a flower of undefined meaning
But it's delightful and precious

Courier from Jia Yi, with rolling waves
Flapped another afternoon that made the flower tremble
And the colours of the mid-autumn moon somewhat stolid
And at a loss

Daily, I sweep the soul
Pruning the adopted rose and replacing it with clean water
I rise and change into a skirt with jasmine fragrance

The rose and the mid-autumn moon
Are hanging on our hearts
It is evasive, as it may
Possibly have dreamed of the mountains, waters and woods outside the
universe

我一低头
某一片遥远的风景，升起
孤独的美，那么纯粹
让人停靠在往事的细节中内疚，灿烂无比

（2009 年 9 月 23 日晨）

As soon as I lower my head
A distant landscape rises
Its solitary beauty so pure
That one stops in the details of the past, feeling guilty, brilliant

(Morning, 23/9/2009)

楼隐

来世，一定要早些遇见
在错过之前
你一定要选择有竹子柳树与湖水的地方
等候我
或者经过江南的古镇
像静物一样楼隐于
某一口古井与茶花的深处
那样，你就不会被别人领走了

当月亮挂在树梢的时候
你搬一把藤椅，为我梳头
用米兰和玉兰的香气
爱我
然后，你的手指和嘴唇
所到我的皮肤之处
景色落下来

你让我住进你词语的厢房
活在一首离你心脏最近的诗中
呼吸你的氧气
两个人的童话
——超现实的美
危险而揪心

如一块江南的石头上
被岁月镂刻下的残文
——"楼隐"
像谜
被后人猜测
抽象了时间

Living in Seclusion

In my next life, we must meet as early as possible
And before we miss each other
You must choose a place with bamboos, willows and a lake
To wait for me
Or pass an ancient town in River South
Living in seclusion, like a still object
In the depths of an ancient well and tea flowers
That way, you won't be taken by someone else

When the moon hangs on a branch
You bring in a rattan chair and comb my hair
With the fragrances of orchid and magnolia
Loving me
And then the scene falls
Wherever your fingers and lips
Touch my skin

You allow me to live inside the wing-room of your words
To be alive in a poem closest to your heart
Breathing your oxygen
A fairy tale for two
—surreal beauty
Dangerous and heart-pinching

Like a River South stone
Carved by time with a fragment
—"棲隐"
Like a riddle
To be guessed at by posterity
With time abstracted

抽象了孤独

（2011年5月29日凌晨1点20分）

And solitude abstracted

(1.20am, 29/6/2011)

退回今生

鱼，我在一万米的高空
捕捉你，离现实很远
离来世很近
那些挂在空中的吻
飘来飘去
接不到你的气息

从前，那个唯一的夜晚
一场盛宴愧对于春色和山水
你在时间中迟到
满身浪潮
把我席卷到天明

依窗望去
端午的月亮又瘦又小
悬在机翼的左边
像避邪一样
饱受冷落

她洒落在人间的月色
在南海争端中羞愧
无常
又在海事威胁中
被敌视

像我一颗心，升到一万米的高处
心酸又博大，不能完全敞开
坐失良机
被你的惶恐、虚弱
误伤

Stepping Back to This Life

Fish, I'm catching you ten thousand meters
High, far from the realities
But close to next life
Kisses, hanging in the air
And adrift
Cannot receive your breathings

In the past, on that only night
With a feast, ashamed of facing the colours of spring, mountains and water
You arrived late in time
A personful of waves
Carried me to dawn

Watching and leaning against the window
The moon of the Duanwu Festival was thin and small
Hanging on the left side of the plane's wing
As if to ward off evil spirits
Having its fill of indifference

The colours of the moon it scattered over the world
Became ashamed and inconstant
In the South China Sea dispute
And suffered hostilities
In the maritime threats

Like my heart, risen to 10,000 meters high
Sad and broad, not completely open
And missing the opportunities
Wounded by your fears
And weaknesses

撕裂
让我从来世惊醒
退回到今生

夜用黑把白天归于零
机窗用一小块玻璃把整个世界归于零
你用走近与挣脱
把我归于零

鱼，这时
我在天上，炉火纯青
用闲云追踪往事
用隐痛冶炼金子

（2011年端午节于飞机上）

And ripped apart
Waking me up from my next life
To come back to this one

Night reduced day to zero with blackness
As the window of the airplane reduced the world to zero with a small glass
And you reduced me to zero
With approaching and shaking free

Fish, now
I'm in the sky, a perfect fire
Chasing after things past, with the leisurely clouds
And smelting gold with hidden pain

(On the airplane, Duanwu Festival, 2011)

距离

你把距离丢进时间的流水
那一刻起
童话就在一株艾草上
落魄
成了两个人的咒语

先前的一念之差
误以为是海阔天空
我从繁华的梦境
走到了绝路
回过头来，岸在哪里

酒后，那些纸上的承诺
只能使梦深情浅
我落叶纷飞的心事
被你用石沉大海推脱
用修辞一一省略

短期内，一些误伤
像雪地上的樱桃
显得辉煌，目空一切
我把自己弃置于全球化的荒野
努力做一个不幸的诗人

然后，在万里浮云之上
令每一个词语放弃抵抗
仔细推敲，每一个句子，每一句话
背靠你，都过于寒冷
夏天路过我的窗户结满了薄冰
你在一首诗中牙痛，被误解

Distance

You chuck distance into the running water of time
And from that instant on
A fairy tale loses its soul
On a blade of wormwood
Becoming a curse for two

An instant thought in the past
Mistook it as vast as the ocean and the sky
But when I walked to the end of the road
From a flourishing dream
And turned my head back, where is the bank?

After wine-drinking, promises on the paper
Managed to make dreams deep and feelings shallow
While my heart matters with flying fallen leaves
Were pushed aside by your stone that sank into the sea
Omitted, one by one, by rhetoric

For a short period of time, a number of accidental injuries
Seemed to be brilliant
Like cherries on the snow, holding everything beneath their notice
I abandoned myself to the globalised wilderness
Trying to be an unfortunate poet

Then, above the floating clouds of ten thousand *li*
I carefully weighed my words, line by line
Even with my back against you, it was too cold
Windows that went past me in summer were covered with a thin ice
You, misunderstood, suffer tooth pain in a poem

世上最隐痛的
缘于两颗心的距离
远处，掠过佳肴柔滑的美味
那是你精心为别人做的
此时
天与地，我与你

（2011年7月3日）

What hurts most in a hidden way, in the world
Is the distance between the two hearts
Far away, sweeps a soft beautiful taste of delicacies
Meticulously made by you for others
And now
The sky and the earth, the I and the you

(3/7/2011)

吹到天上的格桑花

玉树，在四月是暴虐的，决绝的
成为天堂最后的驿站

三江源把人们的心卷进了
7.1级流动的悲伤

结古镇的天空，刺骨
阵阵风沙触到死者的头发和衣角

经幡失去了知觉，
在空旷中默哀

一盏盏点亮的酥油灯
提醒着寒夜中救援的人们

天就要亮了，一身裹满尘土的救援者
没有停止的迹象

狗群闻着来自地狱的尘土
不时跟随在后面恐怖地狂吠

一个牧民的小女儿，梳着麻花辫
从火砖、水泥、钢筋下终于被挖出来

人们聚集在死亡门口
用汉语、藏语抓住她的手拉出鬼门关

走在路上的2046个亡灵回过头来
望着下降的半旗与空中长长的鸣笛

Galsang Flowers, Blown into the Sky

Yushu was violent and resolute in April
Becoming paradise's last post

Sanjiangyuan drew people's hearts into
The running sorrow at 7.1 scale

The sky over Jiegu Town was bone-piercing
Bursts of wind and sand touched the hair and corners of clothes of the dead

Prayer flags, having lost consciousness
Were mourning in the emptiness

Ghee lamps, lit one after another
Served as reminders to the rescuing people in the cold night

The day was about to break but the rescuers, covered with dust
Showed no signs of stopping

Dogs, smelling the dust from hell
Occasionally barked in terror, following them

The young daughter of a herdsman, with twisted pigtails
Was finally dug out of firebricks, cement and steel bars

People were gathering outside the door of Death
Holding her hands, pulled her out of Devil's Pass with Chinese and Tibetan
languages

2046 dead souls on the way turned their heads back
Watching the flags flying at half-mast and long air-raid sirens

审视的眼神如山鹰在凉风中盘旋
吹到天上的格桑花，涂改了死亡

（2010年4月21日）

The scrutinizing eye, like a mountain eagle, was hovering in the cool wind
And the Galsang flowers, blown into the sky, have now tampered with death

(21/4/2010)

愤怒的石头
——祭奠圆明园浩劫150周年

在残山剩水中
我数着劫难死亡
一颗断石的心
存留着150年前暴力的灰烬

1860年耻辱的细节
废墟冷光闪烁，愤怒
斗转星移
人类加速度飞起来
吞食恶果

圆明园让一场火焰
卷入羞耻，卷入伤痛
贪婪弄脏了这个星球
人类，凶猛

抢劫、掠夺、入侵
始终像一把蔓延的大火

在东方
我沦为人类心酸的遗址

（2010年10月8日于北京
2019年4月14日修改）

The Angry Stones

– On the 150 anniversary of the havoc wreaked on the Old Summer Palace

In the remains of mountain and water
I count the deaths in the catastrophe
In the heart of a broken stone
Is kept the ashes of violence 150 years ago

Details of shame in 1860
The ruins shining with a cold light and the fury
Remaining, despite the change of seasons
Humanity is taking flight, at an accelerated speed
Swallowing its own evil fruit

Old Summer Palace was plunged by a fire
Into shame and into wounds
And greed has dirtied this planet
Human beings, ferocious

Robbery, pillage, invasion
Always like a fire spreading

In the East
I have sunken into the remains of human sadness

(Beijing, 8/10/2010 and revised, 14/4/2019)

涠洲岛上

1、低垂的美

甩开脚下的海浪
抬腿，踏上涠洲岛
一条小径通向香蕉林
通向满目低垂的美
阳光欲滴，内心敞开
结果离我很近
抱着绿色的拳头
问好，糖的味道
问好，蜜的味道

2、木瓜 木瓜

木瓜 木瓜——
1、2、3、5、6、7
这不是接头暗语
也不是日落海滩
潮起潮落的周期
是第一次看见木瓜长在树上的人
收紧目光的翅膀
口中念念有词

3、让人羞愧的鱼

一个木盆把海水圈禁在岸边
午餐的阳光落在鲎鱼
硬邦邦的背壳上
貌似海龟的鲎鱼
就要被烹饪

On Weizhou Island

1. Drooping Beauties

Casting off the sea waves underfoot
And raising my feet, to step onto Weizhou Island
A path led to a banana forest
To drooping beauties that filled the eyes
The sunlight was dripping and my heart-door was open
The formed fruit was close to me
Holding their green fists
Greeting, with the taste of sugar
Greeting, with the taste of honey

2. Papaya Papaya

Papaya papaya—
1, 2, 3, 5, 6, 7
This is not a code word
Nor is it the cycle in which the sun sets over the beach
And the tide rises and falls
It's the first time when one spots someone whose papaya is grown on a tree
Gathering the wings of his vision
And muttering incantations

3. Fish that Puts One to Shame

A wooden basin imprisons the sea water on the seaside
The sunlight at lunch is falling on the hard back
Of the horseshoe crabs
Ones that look like sea turtles
Are about to be cooked

火焰嘶嘶地在炉膛叫唤
木盆中沙沙划动的鲨鱼
寂静如初，生死相依
抓起一只，另一只
和赴死的伴侣蹬腿紧贴
不离不弃
海潮退回
他们的身体荡起大海
最后的告别

（2011年11月22日）

The fire, hissing in the stove, is calling
The crabs, scratching in the basin
Are as quiet as in the beginning and cling to each other for dear life
If you pick up one, the other
Holding onto him, about to die, with kicking legs
Never lets go
As the tide recedes
Their bodies set the sea afloat
Their last farewell

(22/11/2011)